DECORATED *in* GLORY

DECORATED *in* GLORY

Church Building in Herefordshire in the Fourteenth Century

Nigel Saul

LOGASTON PRESS

FRONT COVER: Hereford Cathedral crossing tower from the north-west (*photograph © Richard Wheeler*)
BACK COVER: Pembridge church and tower from the north-east (*photograph © Richard Wheeler*)
FRONTISPIECE: Weobley church west doorway, detail (*photograph © Richard Wheeler*)

First published in 2020 by Logaston Press
The Holme, Church Road, Eardisley HR3 6NJ
www.logastonpress.co.uk
An imprint of Fircone Books Ltd.

ISBN 978-1-910839-46-1

Text copyright © Nigel Saul, 2020

All images © Nigel Saul except: p. 40 (L), photograph © Bob Anderson; p. 48 (TOP), photograph © Ian Bass;
p. 33, profile drawings by the late Dr R.K. Morris from 'Pembridge and Mature Decorated Architecture in
Herefordshire', in the *Transactions of the Woolhope Naturalists' Field Club* (Vol. XLII, Part II, 1977), reproduced
by kind permission of the publisher and the family of Richard Morris; p. 10 (L), p. 16 (L & BOTTOM), p. 62
(MIDDLE & BOTTOM), p. 100, p. 107, p. 114, photographs © Gordon Taylor LRPS, by kind permission of the
Chapter of Hereford Cathedral; p. ii, p. 13, p. 14 (L), p. 15, p. 16 (R), p. 17 (L), p. 18, p. 19 (BOTTOM), p. 20, p. 24 (L),
p. 25, p. 35, p. 36, p. 37 (R), p. 40 (R), p. 42, p. 43, p. 49 (TOP L & BOTTOM), p. 53 (BOTTOM L), p. 59 (TOP), p. 70,
p. 76, p. 77 (TOP), p. 78, p. 79 (TOP R & BOTTOM), p. 80, p. 81, p. 88, p. 92 (L), p. 93, p. 97, p. 106, p. 115, p. 116, p. 117,
p. 119 (TOP 2), p. 120, p. 122, p. 124, p. 130, photographs © Richard Wheeler.

Designed and typeset by Richard Wheeler.
Cover design by Richard Wheeler.

Printed and bound in Poland

Logaston Press is committed to a sustainable future for our business, our readers and our planet.
The book in your hands is made from paper certified by the Forest Stewardship Council.

FSC
www.fsc.org
MIX
Paper from
responsible sources
FSC® C105618

British Library Catalogue in Publishing Data.
A CIP catalogue record for this book is available from the British Library.

CONTENTS

ACKNOWLEDGEMENTS

The author is grateful to the Lambarde Fund of the Society of Antiquaries of London for a grant to assist with the costs of travelling to and around Herefordshire visiting churches. The author and publishers together are grateful to the Mortimer History Society and the Marc Fitch Fund for generous grants to assist with the costs of publication of this book. Assistance with the provision of photographs was given by Ian Bass, Philip Hume, Robert Anderson and Richard Wheeler. The staff of Hereford Central Library supplied the author with an image of the old Lingen church from the Walter Pilley Collection. Sally Badham kindly read and commented on a draft of the discussion of church monuments in Herefordshire in chapter 2, and Paul Dryburgh read the whole book in draft. The author is especially grateful to Richard and Su Wheeler of Logaston for taking on the project and to Philip Hume for lending it the support of the Mortimer History Society. The book owes much to the researches of the late Richard Morris, whose 1972 University of London PhD thesis on Herefordshire Decorated still provides a firm foundation on which all later scholars build. The present book places much greater emphasis than Morris on matters of patronage and piety; nonetheless it still owes a great deal to his exemplary analysis of the buildings themselves. A scholar from an earlier generation to whom tribute should be paid is the Herefordshire antiquary, George Marshall (d.1950), whose many articles on Herefordshire churches in the *Transactions of the Woolhope Naturalists' Field Club* afford a model of precise scholarship. Last but not least, my thanks are due to my wife, Jane, who has herself been a pillar of support in this enterprise and who has visited many of the churches with me.

The first in an occasional series of papers for the MHS

Hereford Cathedral from the north-west

PROLOGUE

The first half of the fourteenth century witnessed a great flowering of artistic and architectural endeavour in Herefordshire and the neighbouring areas of the Welsh March. The most prestigious project was the rebuilding of the central and western towers and the side aisles of Hereford Cathedral, transforming the great church, at least externally, into the impressive, Gothic-looking structure we see today. At the same time, a magnificent new aisle was built at Leominster Priory, the county's most important monastery, and existing aisles were rebuilt or chapels added at the three big town churches of Ledbury, Ross-on-Wye and Ludlow. In the countryside, the churches at Pembridge and Kingsland were both lavishly rebuilt, and work on a more limited scale was undertaken at a host of other parish churches and manorial chapels in Herefordshire itself and the southern parts of Shropshire. A notable feature of the more ambitious church building in the two counties was the use of ballflower, a form of decoration which was apparently introduced by a mason who had been trained at Wells and who was to be employed on the central tower of Hereford Cathedral, under construction from no later than 1307.

There were just two periods in the Middle Ages when work in Herefordshire may be said to stand near the forefront of English artistic and architectural creativity. One was the mid-twelfth century, the heyday of Romanesque, when Herefordshire sculptors were executing such masterpieces as the Castle Frome font, the Kilpeck south door, and the Brinsop St George and the Dragon. The other was the period under consideration now, the early fourteenth century, the period of what is called 'Decorated' architecture. In Herefordshire this was to be a golden age of English Gothic. Stretching from the 1290s to roughly the time of the Black Death, and spanning the reigns of the first three Edwards, it saw not only the creation of some remarkable buildings but also the painting of some brilliant stained glass windows, and the commissioning of some magnificent tomb monuments. It is the creative achievement of this period, and the social and religious conditions locally which made it possible, which form the subject of this book.

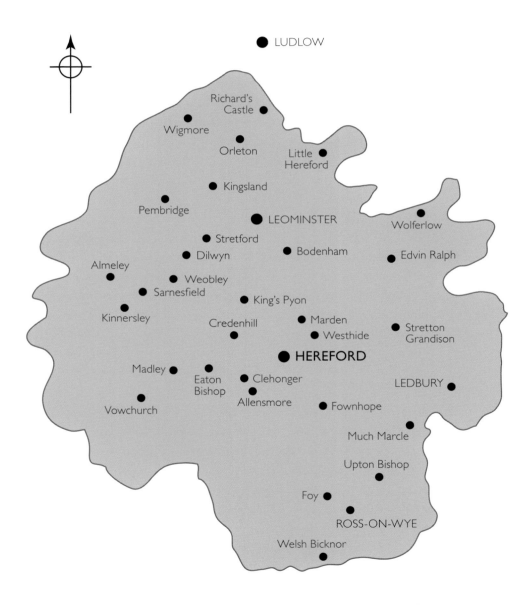

Map of Herefordshire, showing the locations of churches discussed in the text

Herefordshire and the Decorated Style

The county and diocese of Hereford

T HE AREA WHICH was to witness this rich flowering of 'Decorated' architecture corresponded roughly to the boundaries of the medieval diocese of Hereford. The see was one of middling size, straddling the broad pasturelands between its neighbours, the sees of Worcester and Lichfield to the east, and the Welsh border to the west. At its heart was the modern-day county of Hereford, centring on the middle Wye valley and the hills and ridges which cut across it. To the north it took in the uplands of south Shropshire and much of the Severn valley almost as far as Shrewsbury. To the south it extended into the Forest of Dean and pockets of Monmouthshire. To the east a natural boundary was afforded by the Malvern Hills and their outliers, and to the west by the long ridge of the Black Mountains.

The diocese had been established in the late seventh century to minister to the spiritual needs of the so-called Magonsæten, the people dwelling in the western-most parts of the kingdom of Mercia. Its early history is obscure because of the loss of most of the pre tenth-century records, but a cathedral is known to have been established at Hereford by no later than about 900. In the late eleventh and twelfth centuries the first evidence is afforded of the formation of a body of clergy dedicated to serving the cathedral, with a dean at its head, and with lands assigned to its indi-vidual members, the lands that were later to constitute the cathedral's prebends. By 1086, when Domesday Book was compiled, the bishops themselves appear to have accumulated a not insubstantial endowment amounting to some 300 hides. The see was never to be one of the wealthiest in England, scarcely approaching well-endowed Canterbury, Winchester or Durham in resources. What it lacked in lands and rights, however, it more than made up for in antiquity. The long history of the mother church at Hereford was attested by its possession of a magnificent Gospel book dating to the late eighth century. And within its walls were contained the bones of a celebrated local saint, Ethelbert, once the king of East Anglia, who in 794 had been murdered on the banks of the Lugg, just north of the city, on the instructions of his enemy King Offa.

The estates of the see of Hereford were made up of about a dozen-and-a-half manors scattered mostly in the middle and eastern parts of the county and southern Shropshire. The three most valuable properties were the towns of Ledbury, Bromyard and Ross-on-Wye, each worth over £100 per annum and the first-named taking in important outliers at Bosbury, Colwall and Eastnor. Bosbury, just northwest of Ledbury, had a comfortable manor-house which was one of the most favoured residences of the bishops, particularly of Richard Swinfield. Outside the county the bishops also had an important estate at Prestbury, near Cheltenham (Glos), which provided them with a useful staging-post on their journeyings to and from London for meetings of parliament and convocation. The estates of the dean and chapter were also scattered across the eastern and middle parts of the county and included the manors of Breinton, Bullinghope, Withington and Canon Pyon. In addition to being lords of lands and manors, both the bishop and the dean and chapter were holders of advowsons: that is to say, they were patrons of churches to which they appointed the incumbents. In Herefordshire, the bishop had as many as three-dozen churches in his gift, and the dean and chapter between a quarter and a half of that number. By the middle of the thirteenth century the principle had been established that with the right of appointment went the obligation to maintain the church's chancel, the cost of which the advowson holder was expected to bear. Sometimes in the Midlands, at Cotterstock (Northants) for example, we find grand 'Decorated' chancels towering over earlier, relatively insubstantial naves. In Herefordshire, however, this mismatch is not found, and chancel and nave are always kept in due proportion to one another.

In contrast to the powerful presence exerted in the diocese by the cathedral and the dean and chapter, the monasteries figured relatively little in the religious and secular life of the locality. In notable contrast to the position in neighbouring Shropshire and Gloucestershire, there were no Benedictine or Cistercian monastic houses of the first rank. In the north of the county the most important house was Leominster priory, a dependent cell of Reading Abbey, founded on the site of a former minster by Henry I in 1123 and endowed with revenues, mainly in the form of spiritualities, in and around Leominster. At the Dissolution, it enjoyed an annual income of nearly £450, which was exceeded among Marcher monastic houses only by the values recorded for Shrewsbury Abbey and St Werburgh's, Chester.[1] In the south-west of the county there was Abbey Dore, a Cistercian house founded in 1147 by Robert of Ewyas, and for long the burial place of his descendants as lords of Ewyas. Its choir and ambulatory were magnificently rebuilt in the early thirteenth century, probably by masons who had worked at or were familiar with Wells Cathedral and Glastonbury Abbey. In the north-west of the county the most important foundation was Wigmore Abbey, an Augustinian house established by Hugh de Mortimer in the 1130s, and settled first at Shobdon before it was moved to what was to be its permanent site a mile to the north of Wigmore village. As at Abbey Dore to the south, its church was conceived as a mausoleum church, and generations of the Mortimer family were buried within its walls down to the fourteenth century. The remains of the abbey today are disappointingly few. At Wormsley, in the middle of the county, there was a much smaller Augustinian house, but one endowed with a number of local parish churches, and in the fourteenth century its prior was to be involved in the rebuilding of the chancel at Dilwyn. The county's other religious houses, those at Craswall, Aconbury and Limebrook, were all very minor. In the city of Hereford itself the various mendicant Orders were represented, mainly in the suburbs, by small to medium-sized houses.

If the physical presence of the monks on the county was relatively slight, the opposite must be said of those most assertive symbols of secular lordship, the castles and fortified manor houses of the baronial and knightly class. These buildings were all too visible, for Herefordshire, like Shropshire and Cheshire to its north, was a border county, a semi-militarised society, a bastion against the raids and depredations of the Welsh. As early as the reign of Edward the Confessor (1042–66) castles were being built in Herefordshire by Norman settler lords, and by the early thirteenth century, when the age of castle building was drawing to a close, well over three-dozen of these structures were to be counted. Many of them were to fall into decay in the late Middle Ages after the last Welsh principalities were extinguished and the danger of Welsh raids correspondingly reduced, although some were refortified after 1400 at the time of Glyndwr's revolt. Castles, properly called, shaded off into the fortified manor houses of the knightly and lesser gentry class, which were usually moated although lacking in the more demonstrably military character of castles. The large number of evocative earthwork sites in Herefordshire, among them the examples at Moreton-on-Lugg and Mainstone in Pixley, are all that remain today of these often comfortable and well-appointed residences which were usually abandoned in the Tudor period. Across the border in Shropshire, Stokesay Castle near Ludlow affords a rare example of such a manor house that has come down to us largely intact. Many of these properties had private chapels either incorporated into their fabrics or sited nearby in the grounds, and some of these, such as that at Amberley Court near Marden, were rebuilt in the Decorated period. In the windows of the sanctuary at Amberley characteristic Herefordshire Y-shaped tracery is employed, while in the nave the windows have heads with quatrefoils.

The proprietors who lived in these fortified or semi-fortified dwellings fall into two main categories – the higher nobility, who made up the House of Lords in parliament, and the knights and esquires, together comprising the gentry, who along with the burgesses were represented in parliament by the Commons. It is the members of these two groupings whom we see lying on their high tombs in churches, usually with their ladyfolk alongside them, and it is also often they who, in the Decorated period, were responsible for commissioning the rebuilding of the churches in which they were interred.

Wigmore Castle: looking north-east over the ruins

Amongst the most exalted of the higher nobility, much the most important family in Herefordshire and the Central Marches were the Mortimers of Wigmore, a line that could trace its ancestry back to the earliest days of the Conquest. In the early four-teenth century the head of the family was Sir Roger, later the first earl of March, well known as the paramour of Edward II's queen, Isabella, and co-ruler of England with her after the overthrow and death of her husband. Roger's career had something of the roller-coaster about it.[2] Shortly after succeeding his father in 1304, he entered royal service and was initially loyal to the king, acting as his lieutenant in Ireland. By 1320, however, he was growing disaffected, alienated by the ambitions of Edward's favour-ites, the two Despensers, whom he saw as a threat to his interests in the Marches. In 1321, along with other of the Marcher lords, he rose in rebellion, forming an alliance with the northern rebels led by the earl of Lancaster. Separated from the latter, however, and unnerved by Edward's swift advance to the Severn, in January he surrendered to the king at Shrewsbury and was imprisoned in the Tower. Two years later, in 1324 he made a dramatic escape, after drugging his guards, and plotted with the queen to depose her husband. In 1326 the pair returned from exile, Edward's regime collapsed, and the latter's son, the fourteen-year-old Edward III, was enthroned, with Isabella and Mortimer ruling in his name. The couple's regime quickly became as unpopular as that which it replaced, and in 1330 the young king, in a coup d'état at Nottingham, arrested his mother and her lover and had the latter executed.

Roger was in many ways a brilliant and charismatic figure, but he was also a divisive one, alienating many by his rapacity and unscrupulousness. In the course of his nearly four years in power from 1327 he pursued a ruthless policy of territorial aggrandisement and amassed a huge personal fortune. His extreme acquisitiveness, however, may have been driven in part by his initially difficult personal circumstances. When he succeeded in 1304, he was able to enter only a part of his paternal inheritance, well over a half of it being held in dower by his long-lived mother, Margaret, who occupied many of the most important family manors including those of Pembridge and Wigmore itself.[3] Roger was thereby deprived of a very significant part of his potential income. This unfortunate situation, however, was largely counterbalanced by his acquisition from 1308 of the Geneville inheritance, which came to him by his marriage to Joan, daughter and heiress of Geoffrey de Geneville, a wealthy Anglo-Irish lord.[4] It was through this match that the family were to acquire the great castle of Ludlow, over the county border into Shropshire, which by the second half of the century was to supplant Wigmore as the main family seat.

Mortimer power was to suffer further ups and downs on the wheel of fortune in the years after Roger's death. Roger's heir was his son Edmund, who was to die the year after his father, and his heir in turn was to be his son, another Roger, who was a minor, aged three. For the next fifteen years the inheritance was to be taken into custody and broken up, and the family's influence, both locally and nationally, much diminished. Margaret, the first earl's mother, was to continue to hold a large share of the family estates, including Pembridge, in dower until her death in 1334. The late earl's widow, Joan, held the Geneville inheritance in her own right and so occupied Ludlow and the Shropshire lands, while Edmund's own widow, Elizabeth, held many of the family's Welsh lordships in dower. What was left of the inheritance was held by the king for the duration of the minority, and much of it was put out to lease.

The task of putting these scattered pieces back together again fell to the younger Roger when he came of age in the next decade, and in stages in 1346 and 1347 he was allowed possession of all the lands that his father had held at his death. In the course of what was to be a distinguished career he devoted himself to royal service, taking part in Edward III's campaigns in France, fighting valiantly at Crécy and being rewarded in the next year with election as a Founder Knight of the Garter.[5] Roger died, still relatively young, in France in 1360, and his son and heir in turn, another Edmund, was to bring further distinction – and further lands – to the family by marrying Philippa, daughter and heiress of Lionel, duke of Clarence, one of Edward III's younger sons.[6]

The other baronial or semi-baronial families with interests in Herefordshire and the central Marches in this period were all considerably inferior in wealth and standing to the Mortimers. In the early years of the century there were a couple of families whose wealth placed them just inside the baronage, and some way above the gentry: these were the Mortimers of Richard's Castle and the Verdons of Weobley (Heref.) and Alton (Staffs). Both families were to die out in the male line before the middle of the century. In the case of the Verdons, the estates were divided between four co-heiresses, whose husbands' main interests lay elsewhere, with the result that Weobley Castle fell into decay. In the middle of the century, the Grandisons (kinsmen and allies of the wealthy John de Grandison, bishop of Exeter) were to enjoy a brief flowering at their manor house of Ashperton, but politically they subordinated their interests to those of the Mortimers, and Peter, Lord Grandison, was to marry Blanche, daughter of Roger, the first earl.[7]

Herefordshire's three-dozen or so gentry families overlapped at their upper end with the lower rungs of the nobility, some families such as the Devereux of Bodenham sinking from the nobility they had once enjoyed, while others, such as the Grandisons and the Talbots, made the step up. One family, the Chandoses of Fownhope and Snodhill, were honoured with summonses to parliament as titled lords in one generation, but not in the next.

The gentry, principally the knights, were the workhorses of local government in medieval England. They were the people from whom the sheriffs, the keeper of the peace, the escheators and all the other officers who carried the king's government into the shires, were recruited, and likewise those from whom the knights of the shire – the MPs – were chosen to represent their county in parliament. By the fourteenth century we find some knights, such as Sir Roger Chandos and Sir Roger Pychard in Herefordshire, who made something of a career out of serving in local government.[8] Although they were entitled to reclaim any expenses they had incurred, the posts they filled were not salaried, and the main attraction to them of holding office appears to have been the influence that it conferred locally.

If the gentry were on their way to becoming a civilian magistracy, however, they were by no means entirely losing their ancient credentials as men-at-arms. Throughout the first half of the fourteenth century they were still regularly performing military service for the king. Knights from Herefordshire are recorded in the royal pay accounts as serving in Scotland in the early 1300s and in France in the 1340s and 1350s, and three knights at least from the county are known to have shared in the great English victory at Crécy. When we see the knights and barons shown on their high tombs in armour, it was not entirely out of respect for the artistic convention that members of the second estate should be shown in their attire of rank. It was, in part at least, in recognition of the fact that they had actually seen military service.

In another capacity the knights and nobility, like the bishops, were also lords – lords, that is, of manors and men, landed proprietors who relied on the rents and labours of their tenants for the incomes they enjoyed. Without the revenues which they garnered from their landed estates they could hardly have paid for all the churches and chapels they either rebuilt or embellished.

The principal source of wealth for medieval lords, especially those in the Welsh Marches, was agriculture. In most villages in the county and elsewhere in the Midlands a combination of arable and pastoral husbandry was practised, with the balance tilting in the early fourteenth century towards the former under the pressures of a rising population. Typically, a combination of winter- and spring-sown crops was grown. Winter crops might include wheat, rye and maslin, the wheat being grown mainly for sale; and spring crops, barley, oats and legumes, the barley being grown for malting and the oats for winter fodder. In most villages a two- or three-field system of crop rotation was practised, with one field being left fallow each year to allow the soil to recover. Part of the village's acreage was typically held by the lord in demesne – that is, worked as his home farm – while the rest was divided between the tenants, many of whom, by the fourteenth century, would be burdened by the obligation to perform labour services for the lord as part of their rent. In a county such as Herefordshire which had a varied landscape, with hills alternating with river valleys and woodlands, the pastoral economy was also important. On the hills of the Welsh Marches sheep were reared in large numbers, the profits from their clips filling the pockets of their fortunate owners, mainly the lords, while in the river valleys cattle were grazed and in the woodlands pigs allowed to roam. Towns such as Hereford, Leominster and Bromyard prospered as busy market places where cattle and sheep were brought for sale, and Leominster in particular was a significant centre for the wool trade.

Broadly speaking, the economic conditions of the early fourteenth century favoured the lords far more than they did the peasantry. With the population high and continuing to rise, labour was plentiful and wages low, while the market for produce was buoyant, making for high prices. In most years producers could probably enjoy the prospect of reasonable profits. In a harvest-dependent society, however, there was always an element of uncertainty, and in two successive summers in the mid-1310s heavy rain wrought havoc with the crops, leading to serious famine. There was a recurrence of poor weather in the 1320s. It was not until the coming of the plague in 1348, however, that the relationship between supply and demand in the economy was to alter fundamentally, with the collapse in population empowering the lower orders against their superiors, the lords and employers. In the years before then, those years between 1290 and 1348 which saw the great flowering of Decorated architecture in Herefordshire and south Shropshire, it was the lords, the main patrons of building, who were in the ascendant.

It is also worth noting that in these same years England was largely at peace internally, with the notable exception of the six months in 1321–22 when there was a major baronial rising against the Despensers in the Marches. In that sense, the Herefordshire lordly class of the early fourteenth century were in a far better position to exercise architectural patronage than their predecessors in the twelfth century had been, when the talented teams of sculptors whom they employed had been operating for part of the time to the backdrop of a raging civil war in England.

The Decorated Style

The style which we recognise today as 'Decorated' was given its modern-day name in the early nineteenth century by the architectural historian Thomas Rickman, who devised the familiar periodisation of English medieval architecture into Early English, Decorated and Perpendicular.[9] It makes an appropriate enough designation, because the Decorated period constitutes by far the most exuberant phase of English Gothic. While its approximate time of emergence is reasonably clear – the third quarter of the thirteenth century – the time of its ending is much less so. In some parts of the country, notably east Yorkshire, Lincolnshire and around the Wash, Decorated features were to live on until as late as the 1360s or even the 1370s. In the west, however, and in particular in the Severn valley, the change was to come much earlier, in the 1340s and 1350s. In most parts of the country there was an overlap between late Decorated and Perpendicular.

The main characteristics of Decorated were its exuberance, in some cases its extreme decorative richness, and its preoccupation with the creation of highly ornamented, lustrous and burnished interiors. It was a style concerned not so much with structure and architectural form as with surface decoration. Its blanket of rich, decorative coverage was applied equally in three-storey cathedrals, box-like chapels, aisles bolted onto the sides of parish churches, and even solid monastic choirs. Decorated motifs, chief among them ogee arches, ballflower, nichework, foliage and rosette diaper, were deployed with equal enthusiasm on liturgical furniture, shrines, tombs and even memorial crosses, notably the Eleanor Crosses honouring the memory of Edward I's late queen, Eleanor. The same repertory of motifs was drawn on in stained glass, embroideries, ivory carvings, paintings and metal objects, enabling a building to resonate with designs on both the largest and the smallest scales. Much of the finest work of the Decorated period is found in the ornate, micro-architectural treatment of such liturgical fittings as sedilia or piscinas, which dignified them as architectural features in their own right. Little or no unity is to be observed in the creations of the Decorated period. Most buildings constructed in the style consist of additions or extensions to earlier structures, their scale and design often adapted to accommodate an existing matrix. What we are looking at is a series of local architectural endeavours, some of them dazzling, a few of them exotic, but many, the product of limited purses, relatively undistinguished. Examples of all types are to be found in Herefordshire and south Shropshire.

One of the defining characteristics of the Decorated style was its use of bigger windows, large, elaborately traceried openings, which rapidly supplanted the simple lancets characteristic of Early English Gothic. These new windows were an importation from France, where they had been employed in the clerestory of Reims Cathedral, the French coronation church, which was rebuilt from 1211. They were made up of two big main lights, on top of which was placed a cusped oculus. This form of window, using what is called bar tracery, provided the point of departure for all the more varied window types of the Decorated period, ranging from those of Geometrical design, which played with groups of oculi at the top, through to the aptly named Curvilinear forms, which used flowing ogee motifs and were highly popular in the years after about 1320.

The introduction of the new style into England is usually seen as following in the wake of Henry III's rebuilding of Westminster Abbey, which was begun at the east end in 1245. As the abbey, which lay immediately adjacent to the royal palace, was the coronation church of the English kings, it is hardly surprising that it paid due architectural acknowledgement to its French counterpart by borrowing a range of motifs from it, not least its grand new fenestration. Tall traceried windows very similar to those at Reims were used in the abbey both in the choir clerestory and along the aisles, making it a church better lit than any before in England. There were a number of other ways in which Henry III's magnificent new church was to mark a new departure in English architecture. In the outside walls of the triforium gallery, for example, curved triangular windows were used, an exotic window form, the like of which had never before been seen in England. On the inside of the church the surfaces were covered in rich ornament. The spandrels of both the triforium and the main arcade were carved with a trellis-like diaper pattern, which was picked out in gilt against a red background. The vault bosses were carved with foliage and figure sculpture, and the window embrasures and the blind arcading of the aisles and chapels adorned with busts of angels, foliage and figured scenes. The abbey was conceived as a rich, bejewelled reliquary owing something in its decorative conception to another French building, the Sainte-Chapelle in Paris, itself a shrine church. The choir at Westminster was without doubt the most dramatic interior in England, a place of worship transformed into sheer theatre.

Hereford Cathedral: interior of North Transept, showing window tracery and arcade

The architectural reaction to Westminster was surprisingly muted, at least to begin with. At only three other major churches – the cathedrals of Lichfield, Hereford and Salisbury – was there any direct acceptance of the architectural and non-figurative innovations seen at the abbey. It was at Hereford, in the magnificent new north transept built by Bishop Pierre d'Aigueblanche (d.1268), a courtier cleric of Savoyard origin, that by far the most dramatic borrowings were made. As in the choir and transepts at Westminster, rich diaper work was employed to decorate the spandrels of the new triforium. In the aisle windows and the triforium openings the tracery takes the form of the three-light and three-circle type adopted in the late 1250s in the north walk of the cloister at Westminster. And in the clerestory, curved triangular windows were used of precisely the kind that illuminated the triforium gallery at Westminster. It is also possible to detect a Westminster borrowing in the astringent, almost straight-sided arches of the two-bay east arcade, which are the result of imitating the tall Westminster arcade without having the height to accommodate it. The extraordinary north transept at Hereford was too alien in style to exert any influence locally in Herefordshire and the Marches. Moreover, imitating the level of its decoration would have involved any patron attempting it in expenditure way beyond the means available to most local proprietors. The Hereford north transept was to remain an isolated masterpiece, a brilliant and exotic borrowing, but an architectural dead-end.

It was not so much Westminster and its immediate imitators that were to be influential in the dissemination of the new style as a second generation of buildings under construction from the late 1250s.[10] These were all more eclectic in their borrowings, embracing those elements which were acceptable to English taste while rejecting others that smacked of French inspiration. The first and perhaps most important of this series of buildings was the big eastern arm, the so-called 'new work', of Old St Paul's Cathedral, begun in the 1250s but destroyed in the Great Fire of 1666. This extension was a huge structure, twelve bays long, known to us from seventeenth-century drawings and engravings, most notably those of Wenceslaus Hollar. The windows of the aisles and clerestory followed those of Westminster in being of three lights with oculi above, and there was a big Westminster-inspired rose window in the east wall. These features apart, however, most elements of the design had their origins in English architecture of the previous generation, for example in the long eastern arm of Ely Cathedral.

A second major work undertaken in this period, almost contemporaneously with that at St Paul's, was the construction of the Angel Choir at Lincoln (1256–80), an eastern extension of St Hugh's choir, intended in part as a setting for the saint's shrine. This is a highly ornate structure which takes its delight in surface richness from Westminster and also adopts the Westminster idea of placing sculpted angels in the spandrels of the triforium. As at Old St Paul's, however, most elements of the design were firmly traditional in character, the three-storey elevation conforming closely to that of the choir and nave further west, and the clustered piers and delight in foliage sculpture owing much to Ely. The works at Lincoln were to have a considerable impact on local parish church architecture in Lincolnshire and Nottinghamshire. The influence of the cathedral was to be felt further afield, however, with the rebuildings at the collegiate churches of Ripon and Howden in Yorkshire owing much to its example.

As is apparent from the evolution of architectural style in the east and north-east of England, the unfolding of Decorated in the late thirteenth and early fourteenth centuries was to take a highly regional turn. Decorated churches in Yorkshire have a different look from churches in that style in Norfolk and Suffolk, and these in turn look different from their counterparts in the Thames Valley. In the west of England the churches of the period have a different look again. At Exeter Cathedral, rebuilt from end to end except for the towers between the 1270s and the 1360s, the emphasis was on linear richness, a particular delight taken in the seemingly endless multiplication of column shafts and vaulting ribs. In Somerset, at the cathedral and the bishop's palace at Wells, where a programme of works was inaugurated in the 1280s by the wealthy courtier bishop, Robert Burnell, Edward I's chancellor, there was likewise a preoccupation with surface decoration and the multiplication of shafts and ribs. At Wells far more than at Exeter, however, the vocabulary of motifs was extended to include the decorative possibilities of gables and more varied forms of window tracery. Prominent among the tracery forms at Wells are cusped oculi, intersecting lights, spherical triangles and pointed trefoils. The works at Wells were to be of considerable importance in the spread of Decorated to Herefordshire, because Wells mouldings and motifs turn up in the parts of Hereford Cathedral rebuilt from the 1290s. In all probability, it was a mason who had been trained at Wells who was recruited to take charge of the works at Hereford.[11] For this reason, it is worth giving a moment or two's consideration to the essential characteristics of this mason's style.

The first phase of the programme of works at Wells focused on the rebuilding of the hall of the bishop's palace, just to the south of the cathedral, and the construction off it of an exquisite private chapel. In the tracery of the easternmost lateral bays of the chapel a highly distinctive motif was to be employed: the unframed pointed trefoil. This same motif, an innovative one, was to be employed at Hereford a decade later, in the windows of the aisles of the choir and nave, and around 1318, by another mason, in the heads of the chancel windows at Madley (*see pp. 22–23*). As soon as the works on the chapel were complete, the centre of operations switched to the opposite side of the cathedral, where a magnificent new chapter house was constructed. This took the form of a big octagonal building, constructed at first-floor level around a central pier from which the vaulting ribs all radiated. On the surrounds of the windows and on the frames of the seating below, the ornament known as ballflower was employed, apparently for the first time in the west of England. Some ten to fifteen years later, ballflower, like the pointed trefoil, was to be employed at Hereford, in this case on the decoration of the central tower, which was under construction from no later than 1305. It was on the Hereford tower that ballflower was to make its first appearance in the West Midlands and the Marches (*see pp. 16–18*).

The programme of works initiated at Hereford, which followed hard on the heels of those at Wells, began fairly modestly, but over time grew in ambition. Bishop

Hereford Cathedral from the north, showing the north nave aisle window tracery

Swinfield, the man principally responsible, does not appear, initially at least, to have contemplated a full end-to-end rebuilding of his cathedral. After commissioning a grand new entrance portal on the north side of the nave, to improve access, there are signs that he paused for a while. But then in the 1290s he embarked on remodelling the side aisles along the full length of the building, so as to create a grand processional way from west to east. Once that job was completed, and after funds had built up again, he went further, initiating the construction of two new eastern transepts. Around 1307 the bishop's ambitions advanced still further, and he embarked on rebuilding the central tower, commissioning a rich repertory of motifs for its surfaces, to proclaim his cathedral's importance to the outside world. His final project, undertaken in the 1310s, was the rebuilding of the western tower, which rose over the far end of the nave.[12] Work on this last project was probably approaching completion by the time of the bishop's death in 1317.

In all, this programme of works must have extended over some 30 years. On stylistic evidence, it seems that the mason from Wells arrived during the later stages of the aisles' remodelling (c.1307–10) and remained in the cathedral lodge until the entire project was finished. Once his commitments at Hereford were over, he appears to have moved on to the Severn valley to undertake commissions at the abbeys of Gloucester and Tewkesbury. At Gloucester the south aisle of the nave, with its profuse ballflower decoration, bears a distinct similarity to the work at Hereford. By the time the mason left Hereford, other masons were being drawn into the area to undertake commissions not only at the cathedral but also in and around the county. To judge from his style, at least one of these men, a mason working at Kingsland, haled from the south-west – in his case, from Bristol. Others, however, appear to have come from the central or north Midlands. In their different ways these men, like their predecessors, were to leave their distinctive mark on the architecture of the county, investing its buildings with a look that marked them out from buildings in other parts of the country.

In essence, the buildings of the Decorated period in Herefordshire may be said to be characterised by two or three main features. The first is the relative simplicity of the window tracery used in most of the smaller churches in the county. While it is true that in the larger or more prestigious buildings quite complex forms were employed – pointed trefoils in the cathedral, elongated quatrefoils at Ledbury, encircled cinquefoil stars at Leominster Priory – in more modest churches one or other of two much simpler forms is usually found. One such is so-called Y-tracery, that is, two main lights separated by a mullion that divides at the top so as to create a small light that might or might not be cusped; the other is three stepped lancets

Y-shaped tracery: plain at Weobley (*left*) and cusped at Allensmore (*right*)

Reticulated tracery in the head of the west window at Pembridge

grouped under a super-arch. Examples of such window types are legion; those at Allensmore, Bodenham, Clehonger and Weobley may be mentioned as typical. In the second quarter of the century another form widely employed in the county was reticulated tracery, so called from its net-like pattern, which is to be found at, among other places, Pembridge and Madley.

The second main feature of Herefordshire Decorated is the intense use made in several of the region's bigger churches of ballflower decoration, a form of ornament consisting of three petals enclosing a ball (*see overleaf*). At the cathedral it was employed on both of the towers, with particular exuberance on the central one which survives, and on the tomb recesses of members of the Swinfield family in the north-east transept and retrochoir. It was also employed with gusto on the windows of the south aisle at Leominster Priory and the north transeptal chapel at Ledbury, both of them works closely related to the cathedral. Less extravagant examples of ballflower are to be seen on arches and doorways at Weobley and Richard's Castle, where in each case it was used to denote features of high status. The ballflower conceit is also often employed on the low tomb recesses which are such a feature of local commemorative art, for example on those at Dilwyn and Upton Bishop. While ballflower ornament is found in a number of other parts of the country, notably in the Thames valley and Lincolnshire, nowhere is it such a defining feature of local architecture as it is in Herefordshire.

Herefordshire Ballflower

The term ballflower describes a form of architectural decoration resembling a ball enclosed in a globular three-petalled flower, generally set into a concave running mould. It is different from much of the profuse foliage sculpture of the Decorated period in that it is of a stylised form, and is not based on direct observation as are the famous leaves of Southwell. A certain resemblance is to be found to the globeflower (*trollius europaeus*), and analogies have also been drawn with half-opened rosebuds. It is not known, however, if generally any attempt was made by the sculptors to reproduce a particular flower-type.

Far left: Ballflower

Left: Globeflower

Below: Detail of Hereford Cathedral tower

Above: window mullion at Ledbury.
Right: The west doorway at Weobley

The earliest recorded use of ballflower in the west of England appears to have been in the chapter house of Wells Cathedral (1286–c.1306), where it is found on the window surrounds and square frames enclosing the seating below. From Wells the conceit was carried to Hereford, where it was extensively employed on the central tower of the cathedral to create a shimmering effect dematerialising the solidity of the structure and evoking an image of the celestial city. By the 1310s and 1320s the device was being carried to other sites in Herefordshire on which cathedral masons were employed, chief among these Leominster Priory, the north chapel of Ledbury church and, over the county border into Shropshire, St Laurence's, Ludlow, where it appears on the north aisle.

Detail of the sedillia canopies at Madley

The craze for ballflower was a brief but intense one. The device is found at its most luxuriant on the south aisle of Gloucester Abbey (now Gloucester Cathedral), another Hereford-influenced work, known to have been under construction by 1318. In the Thames Valley it was employed in the same year on the tomb of Prior Alexander Sutton in St Frideswide's Priory, Oxford (now Christ Church Cathedral). The heyday of ballflower was to come in the 1320s, when it was employed in a host of churches in the Thames and Cherwell valleys of Oxfordshire, and in the Severn valley around Gloucester. An especially rich example of its use is found in the superb north chapel of Badgeworth church near Gloucester. By the 1330s the heyday of ballflower was well over, although late examples can be found, including an early fifteenth-century example, much heavier in form, on the porch of Chipping Norton church (Oxon).

The great attraction of ballflower was the immense impression of richness and encrustation that it lent to a building. The seemingly endless reproduction of the device on towers, doorways or window surrounds both dazzled the onlooker and enhanced the dignity of the structure on which it was employed. While its use undoubtedly added to the expense of a building, the cost could easily be absorbed by elite patrons in an age when labour, especially unskilled labour, was cheap. The rise in the cost of labour after the Black Death was probably a major factor in its decline.

The final feature that may be said to characterise Herefordshire Decorated is a feeling for space. This is something experienced most strongly at two churches in the west of the county, those at Pembridge and Kingsland, and one in the north – Bodenham – where in each case a relatively monumental arcade was employed with the piers spaced widely apart so as to open up views into the aisles. The same sense of airiness is also felt at some of the bigger town churches, notably those at Ledbury and Ross-on-Wye, both of which have tall arcades and big aisles. An interest in spatial perspectives is a notable feature of the Decorated style more generally, although it is usually experienced more in cathedrals than in parish churches, and it often involved playing with polygonal spaces, as at Wells. It probably had its origins in the mendicant architecture of the period, as the friars had an obvious need for naves with big unimpeded spaces to ensure the audibility of the sermons in which they specialised. A further connection with mendicant architecture is found in the use of distinctive roundel, or porthole, windows of the kind found at Pembridge and Kingsland, these being a feature of mendicant architecture in southern Europe, where they were often employed above a tall arcade.

Taken together, these features invest Herefordshire Decorated architecture with a character all of its own, and set it somewhat apart from the styles and repertory of motifs commonly used in

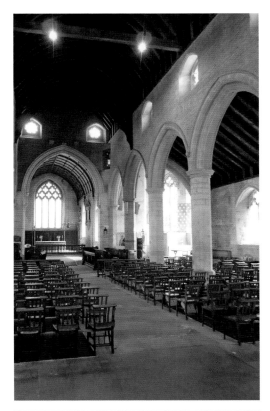

The spacious interiors at Pembridge (*top*) and Ross-on-Wye (*bottom*), both with lofty arcades

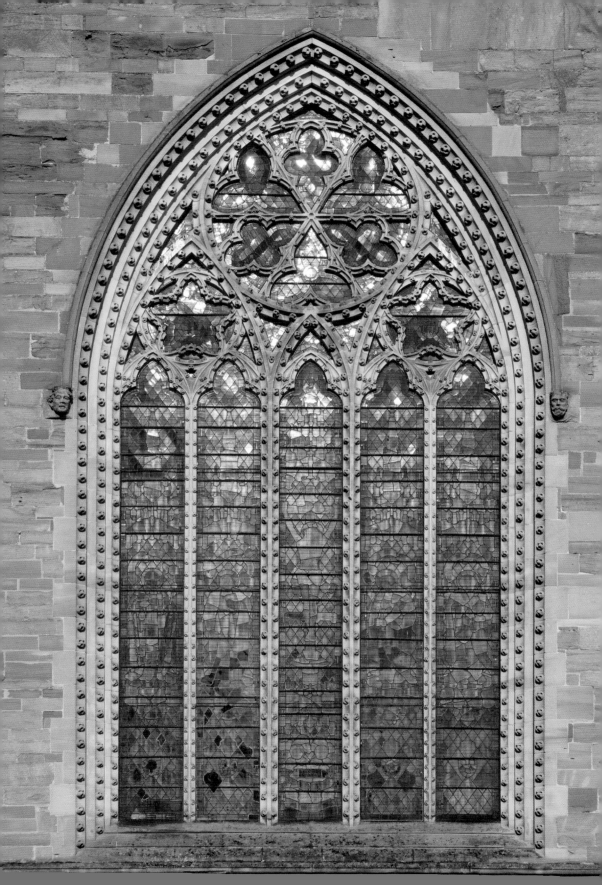

other parts of the country. On the whole, Herefordshire Decorated may be said to be relatively simple in form by comparison. In Herefordshire there was little of the flamboyance that was to be the hallmark of Decorated in some other parts of southern or eastern England. It was only in their enthusiastic use of ballflower decoration that Herefordshire masons were tempted to show off. Nowhere in England are there windows quite so encrusted with the ornament as those at Ledbury or Leominster. While ballflower is commonly encountered in Oxfordshire, for example at Dorchester Abbey, Taynton and Ducklington, it is rarely used with such intensity as it is in Herefordshire. And in no other part of the country, moreover, is it used so frequently to decorate tomb recesses.

The delight taken by the masons in ballflower ornament, however, stands alone as an example of showiness in Herefordshire. Window tracery, as we have seen, is with a few exceptions fairly chaste and unadventurous. In Herefordshire we find none of the fascination shown by the masons of Lincolnshire and the Thames valley in exploring the possibilities of ogee arches, flower petal motifs and swirling mouchettes or soufflets. There is no window in Herefordshire to compare with those at Witney (Oxon) or Shottesbrooke (Berks.) in which inverted trefoil falchions interpenetrate the heads of the main lights. Nor in Herefordshire is there any sign of the inventiveness that was to drive the masons and glaziers at Dorchester Abbey (Oxon) to experiment with spreading a Tree of Jesse across both the glass of the window and the stonework in which it was set. On the other hand, it has to be said that scarcely anywhere in English parish church architecture is there a sight quite so thrilling as that of the Chilston aisle at Madley with its wonderful row of five big windows, all of them with bold reticulated tracery (see overleaf).

The Jesse window at Dorchester Abbey (Oxon)

Opposite: the south aisle east window at Leominster, richly studded with ballflower
Overleaf: the Chilston aisle at Madley, with its memorable sequence of reticulated windows

In a sense, it is easier to say what Herefordshire Decorated is not than what it is. There are few occasions when Herefordshire architecture becomes showy, ostentatious, self-indulgent or capricious. When a Herefordshire mason alighted on a particular window form that he liked, typically he stuck with it; he rarely experimented further. Nor is there any evidence that Herefordshire masons were tempted into elaborating high-status liturgical fittings such as sedilia and piscinas. In no Herefordshire church are there any examples of chancel fittings to compare in sophistication with those in Lincolnshire or Nottinghamshire, outstanding among them the sedilia at Hawton (Notts). Nor can Herefordshire Decorated be described as in any way playful or experimental. It was only in the 1320s, when a Bristol-trained mason arrived in the county, to work at Kingsland, that such conceits as stellate arches – arches made up of big concave elements – made their appearance in the county: and then only in one church (see p. 42).

Left: sedilia in the south aisle at Leominster. *Right*: the far richer sedilia at Hawton in Nottinghamshire

The appeal and fascination of Herefordshire Decorated is found principally in its universality, its adoption in the fourteenth century as the appropriate architectural vocabulary for local church building, adapted as and when necessary to suit local circumstances, and scaled up or down as need be to suit the needs of patrons. Much of what made the county's Decorated-period churches so striking is now lost

The c.1330–35 east window at Eaton Bishop, containing the finest Decorated glass in Herefordshire

to us – the vivid paintings that once spread over the walls, the stained glass that once filled the traceried windows, and all the screens and fittings that marked out how the internal spaces were used. Where some or all of these features survive, they make the world of difference to our appreciation of the interiors. At Eaton Bishop, for example, the survival of the superb stained glass in the east window affords a powerful reminder of how jewel-like a fourteenth-century chancel interior would have looked. At Pembridge the like survival of some of the painted scheme on the walls of the south transept provides an insight into just how bright and colourful even quite modest interiors might once have been (*see p. 119*). All too often interiors that are today scraped and bare compel us to concentrate our attention on the architectural lineaments of a building, where contemporaries might have been struck more by the furnishings and decoration.

The flowering of Decorated in Herefordshire in the early fourteenth century was the product of a quite specific set of social, religious and economic circumstances that made possible a remarkable upsurge in building at this time. It is the scale of that building and the identity of the masons involved in it that call for consideration next. After that, we can move on to the circumstances that brought the great building boom about.

2

Building and Builders

P ROBABLY AS MANY as a half of all Herefordshire's churches survive in their present form essentially as fabrics built in the period between c.1290 and the third quarter of the fourteenth century. Intense church building took place in these years in other parts of the Midlands and West Country, notably in the Severn Valley, central Somerset, south Staffordshire and Cheshire. Nowhere, however, was quite so much building undertaken, nor that building activity quite so widely distributed, as in Herefordshire and the neighbouring areas of south Shropshire. And nowhere have quite so many fabrics of the period come down to us for the most part almost unaltered. In Gloucestershire, Somerset and, to a large extent, in Cheshire a large number of churches were to be rebuilt again in the fifteenth and early sixteenth centuries, with the result that much of the earlier work was obliterated. Away from the Midlands and West Country, only in eastern England, and particularly in Lincolnshire and the lower Trent valley, was church building undertaken on a scale to approach that in Herefordshire. And only in this part of the country have quite so many fabrics survived largely intact.

The buildings in or close to Herefordshire, either constructed or reconstructed in this period, embrace some of the very grandest in the locality and also some of the most humble. At one end of the spectrum is Hereford Cathedral, the focal-point of architectural and artistic endeavour in the central Marches, and at the other, the humble chapel of Amberley Court, a country manor house near Marden. In between lie innumerable parish churches and chapels, the great majority of them in the countryside, but a sizeable minority in the towns, such as Ledbury and Ross-on-Wye.

The pattern of building

The biggest and most prestigious project in the area was, of course, the part-rebuilding of Hereford Cathedral. Launched in the 1280s, this saw what was essentially still a Romanesque structure turned, at least externally, into a mainly Gothic one.[1] The

A seventeenth-century engraving by the German artist Wenceslaus Hollar, showing Hereford Cathedral from the north, and the now-lost spire and twin west towers

first stage in the process was the building of a new entrance portal – what is now the inner north porch, contained within Bishop Booth's later outer porch. This was followed in the 1290s, on Bishop Swinfield's initiative, by a much bigger scheme, the comprehensive remodelling of the cathedral's aisles, for which, as we have seen, a mason who had received his training in Bishop Burnell's service at Wells was recruited. The aisles of the nave were tackled first, followed after an interval by those of the choir, with work on the north side preceding that on the south as it constituted the main access route. Shortly after this, in turn, a beginning was made on a third project, the construction of two new eastern transepts, with the northern one given priority as Bishop Swinfield intended it as his and his family's burial place. The final stages of the programme saw the reconstruction of the cathedral's two towers, work on the central one beginning in about 1305, with its western twin

Hereford Cathedral from the north-west

following in the 1310s. By the 1320s, after some 30 years' near-continuous building, work on the cathedral ground to a halt, probably because of a shortage of money, and the south-eastern transept was left unfinished. Work was to pick up again in the 1360s, after the Black Death, when the incomplete transept was finished and a lavish new chapter house built. This last structure was badly damaged in the fighting in the Civil War and was pulled down in 1769.

After the cathedral, some of the most important building projects were undertaken in the towns. At Hereford itself two of the city's five parish churches, All Saints and St Peter's, were largely rebuilt, in each case with a tall spire, and at the former with a Lady Chapel included on the north side. At Ledbury the whole of the south aisle and the westernmost parts of the north aisle were rebuilt, and a spectacular outer north chapel added. At Ross-on-Wye the south aisle was rebuilt with a ballflower frieze running along the eaves, and a porch was added to the north aisle. At Leominster Priory the parish nave on the south side of the church was rebuilt in the form of a big six-bay aisle, adorned with magnificent traceried windows all studded with ballflower. At Bromyard new fenestration was provided, although otherwise the substantially Romanesque church was left largely untouched.

In the countryside there were a small number of medium-scale end-to-end rebuildings. The most impressive of these was the fine new church at Pembridge, a fluent exercise in mature Decorated, with north and south transepts, a widely-spaced nave arcade, and distinctive circular windows in the clerestory. Only slightly inferior in size was the church at Kingsland, rebuilt in the 1320s and 1330s, this time with pseudo-transepts in the form of gabled east bays, and a porch and attached chantry chapel on the north side. At Weobley and Madley, again sizeable structures, the churches were rebuilt in stages, in the latter case with an apsidal east end over a crypt and a spectacular long outer south aisle, the Chilston aisle (*see pp. 22–23*). At Marden, just to the north of Hereford, the chancel was likewise rebuilt in apsidal form, although in this case on a more modest scale than at Madley.

Numerous smaller parish churches were all but rebuilt, the best and most complete surviving examples being those at Almeley, Ashperton and Stretton Grandison. At Almeley the rebuilding took place in two stages, the chancel first, and the nave a generation later. More common than end-to-end rebuildings were piecemeal works: an aisle added here or a porch and side chapel there. Examples of aisles added to naves are found at Bodenham, Kinnersley and Much Cowarne. At Kingstone and Fownhope small, existing aisles were widened, perhaps to accommodate chantry foundations. At Brinsop the addition of a new aisle was accompanied

Chelmarsh church: the east window

by a westwards lengthening of the nave. Many examples are found of side chapels being added to churches, either in the form of flanking chapels or as transepts set at right angles to the main building. Particularly impressive are the transeptal chapels at Clehonger and Dilwyn, both of which are placed on the north side, and at Letton and King's Pyon, on the side opposite. Sometimes, as at Fownhope and Kinnersley, work started in a limited way on one part of the fabric was followed a few years later by work on another, leading in the end to a near-total rebuilding.

Outside Herefordshire there was substantial church building in neighbouring Shropshire, where new aisles and transepts were built at the big town church at Ludlow and an impressive side chapel added to the country church at Alberbury. At both Shifnal and Stottesdon the chancel was lavishly rebuilt, and at the latter church an aisle chapel added to the south side of the nave. There were two end-to-end rebuildings in Shropshire, one, a modest example, at Neen Sollars, undertaken probably before 1300, and the other, more ambitious, at Chelmarsh where the work can be dated to the mid-1340s. West of Herefordshire, in the Marcher lordships, the church at Crickhowell was completely rebuilt to a cruciform plan shortly before 1300.

Builders and building teams

It is tempting to wonder who were the master masons, or architects as they would be called today, who were responsible for executing all these commissions. In many cases, particularly where the cathedrals are concerned, the names of these men have come down to us in either the contracts into which they entered with their clients or the account rolls in which those clients recorded payments to them. Unfortunately, the name of not one of the masons who worked in Herefordshire in this period is attested in any surviving document – not even that of the master who was recruited from Wells to work at Hereford. Failing a documentary discovery, therefore, the identity of these craftsmen must forever be lost to us.

If we cannot assign a name to any of the men, however, we can at least follow in their footsteps as they moved from church to church in the course of their work. It was usual in the Middle Ages for masons to develop particular stylistic traits, particular mannerisms, which they would repeat over and over again with only minor variations in all the commissions they undertook. Typically, these signature traits reveal themselves most clearly in the moulding profiles and other forms of detailing that the men used on such features as doorways and window jambs (*see overleaf*). By carefully recording these formations and grouping together like examples, we can identify and track the work of particular masons or teams of masons. It should be stressed that the analysis and grouping of mouldings profiles is by no means a precise science. Formations might not in every case be unique to an individual, and sometimes a mason or craftsman is found using patterns very similar to those of someone else, perhaps the man who had first trained him. Nonetheless, in theory, it should still be possible to identify the work of particular teams or schools of masons in a locality, even if we cannot reliably track the work of an individual practitioner. Short of actually discovering the men's names, the analysis of profiles offers by far the most effective means of identifying and tracking the masons who worked on the churches in a locality. It is by application of this methodology that we are able to trace both the arrival of Decorated in Herefordshire and its dissemination from the cathedral to other church sites in the area.

Mouldings in Herefordshire

The study of moulding profiles was pioneered by Richard Morris, whose early work involved close architectural study of the important corpus of early fourteenth-century buildings in Herefordshire and south Shropshire. The key assumption which informed Morris's work was that the hand of each mason or craftsman might reveal itself in the particular mouldings, or profile designs, which he habitually used for such features as pillars, column bases, doorways and, to a certain extent, ribs and mullions. As another writer was to put it, details of this sort 'reveal the hand of the architect much as brush-work does that of the painter'.

As Morris himself would have been the first to admit, the study of mould-ing profiles is rarely as straightforward as it might seem. Archaism might sometimes play a role in deciding the particular choices that men made. In Exeter Cathedral many of the mouldings in the nave, which was rebuilt in the 1330s, correspond closely to those created for the east end, which was built nearly half-a-century earlier. Elsewhere, difficulty might be experienced in establishing close correspondence between the profiles used in buildings which in other ways might be sufficiently similar to one another to suggest that they were designed by the same mason. Designs were never identical across buildings, and adaptations were made to take account of setting and context. In a number of big buildings, cathedrals for example, there is the additional problem that teams of masons were employed, each practitioner broadly following the designs of the overall master, but adapting them to suit his own individual style. In this sort of situation, identifying the trademarks of a particular mason or masons becomes virtually impossible.

When we turn from large-scale buildings to smaller ones – to parish churches for example – problems of this kind pose much less of a difficulty. Here, no more than one main mason at a time is likely to have been employed, and a reasonable hope might be entertained of tracing plausible patterns across buildings. A couple of examples can be given to illustrate this point. In north-west Herefordshire we find a particularly distinctive capital form employed in the early fourteenth-century nave at Pembridge, which is found at four other churches all near Pembridge and nowhere else in the county (*see opposite*). This concentration of examples suggests that the design of the capital was the invention of one mason who was employed in the area, and

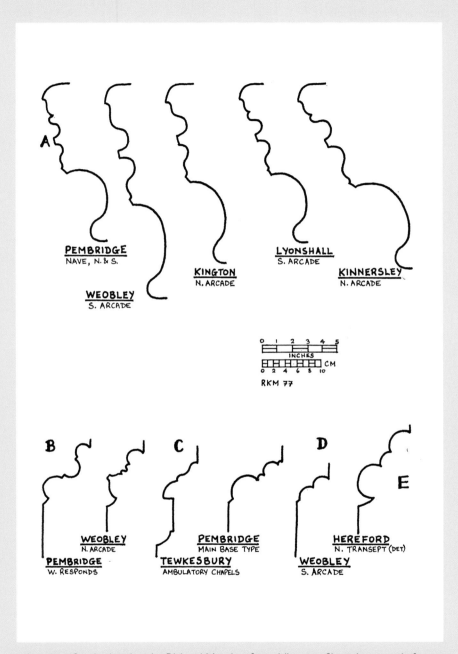

A series of scale drawings by Richard Morris, of mouldings profiles taken mostly from Herefordshire churches, with arcade profiles at the top and base profiles below

that he was responsible for the design of all the buildings in the group. The work of another mason who had a highly distinctive trademark can be identified in a group of churches in the Wye valley west of Hereford. At Madley, the grandest of the group, on the exterior window jambs of the Chilston aisle we find mouldings which consist of pairs of splayed chamfers of equal length separated by a triangular recess made up of a right-angled isosceles triangle. Precisely the same profile can be found on the exterior jambs of the windows at the two neighbouring churches of Eaton Bishop and Allensmore, indicating that the same mason worked on all three.

Comparative photographs of the exterior window jamb mouldings found on three Herefordshire churches a few miles apart: from left to right, Madley (Chilston aisle), Allensmore and Eaton Bishop, showing the near-identical profiles of the surrounds

The study of moulding profiles has proved controversial partly because if used without caution it can lead to the drawing of unwarranted conclusions, and partly because it runs the risk of undervaluing the importance of connoisseurship. It is a methodology, nonetheless, which can yield significant insights in a field of study for which documentary sources at parish church level are disappointingly few.

According to Richard Morris, who made a detailed examination of Herefordshire church architecture in the early fourteenth century, virtually all the main commissions undertaken in churches in or near Herefordshire between c.1300 and 1340 were the work of some four or five masons or teams of masons, the most accomplished of whom were schooled in the architectural styles of the cathedral.[2] Crucial to Morris's interpretation was the work of the master mason who, he believed, had been recruited from Wells to be principal architect of the aisles and towers at the cathedral and who, once his commitments at Hereford were over, apparently moved on to work in the Severn valley, notably at Gloucester and Tewkesbury. It was this man, Morris believed, who was responsible for shaping what was to be the distinctive architectural style of both the cathedral and the diocese of Hereford. Morris's findings, although they have been subsequently amended in detail (not least by Morris himself in his later work), remain essentially unchallenged and provide the foundation for all later writing on Decorated architecture in Herefordshire.[3]

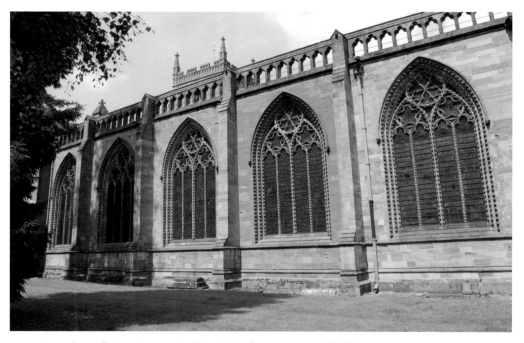

Leominster Priory: the south aisle with its fine sequence of ballflower-encrusted windows

The three churches in Herefordshire on which the styles and motifs developed by the cathedral mason exerted the most direct influence are those at Leominster, Weobley and Ledbury.[4] At Leominster, the great south or parish aisle is one of the show-pieces of Herefordshire Decorated, with its big west window and enfilade of five south windows all identical, their jambs, mullions and tracery encrusted with ballflower. It is the ballflower decoration that constitutes the most obvious link between the Leominster work and that at Hereford, but the similarities do not end there. The Leominster tracery design is based very closely on that of the central tower at the cathedral, its basic idea of two pairs of lights surmounted by a roundel with alternating trefoils and quatrefoils reproducing that of the lights on the tower's upper stage. There are similarities too between the mouldings used at Leominster and those at Hereford. The Leominster aisle may in turn be linked with yet another important Decorated work in the area, the south aisle of Gloucester Abbey (now Cathedral): in the window heads of both buildings is found the same distinctive motif of radiating trefoils and triangles. It seems reasonable to infer that the same man – perhaps the lead Hereford mason – was the mastermind behind both works. Since the Gloucester south aisle is known to have been begun in 1318, the Leominster project can probably be dated to shortly after that.

At Weobley too it is the use of ballflower that provides the most obvious link with the rebuilding at the cathedral. The distinctive bulbous decoration is found on the surrounds of the west door, both outside and in, and on the east arch of the

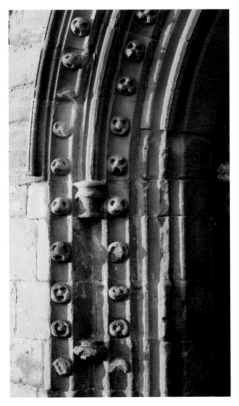

Weobley: the west doorway, with detail on left

north arcade, where it serves to highlight the entrance to the former Lady Chapel. A further link with the cathedral is provided by the mouldings of the nave arcade arches and the interior frame of the west door, which consist of large hollows flanked by broad fillets, a pattern very close in design to that of the mullions and window jambs of the cathedral tower.

Ledbury: the north chapel, west elevation with doorway (*left*) and east elevation (*right*)

At Ledbury the magnificent north chapel provides a close rival to the Leominster south aisle for showy magnificence, with its five majestic windows again all encrusted with rich ballflower decoration. The chapel doorway too is an outstanding work, its mouldings delineated by rose heads and rows of tiny sprigs of foliage, all carved in exquisite detail. As at Leominster and Weobley, the mouldings and other details employed provide direct links with the corresponding formations at the cathedral, particularly with the jambs of the central tower, and a direct link to Weobley itself is provided by the doorway, the forms of which are similar to those on the Weobley west door. At Ledbury, however, influences from important buildings in the north Midlands are also detectable, notably the use of tracery patterns which can be linked to those at the cathedrals of Lichfield and Chester. The last features point to a slightly later date for the Ledbury chapel, perhaps in the 1330s.

Three final works which can be linked to this group are the north aisle of Ludlow, the south aisle of Richard's Castle, and the chancel at Marden. At the first two the link is provided yet again by the delight taken in the use of ballflower, and at the last by the appearance of window tracery forms derived ultimately from the cathedral but mediated probably through Ludlow. If it is reasonable to suppose that the same mason was employed on designing both buildings, it should also be said that

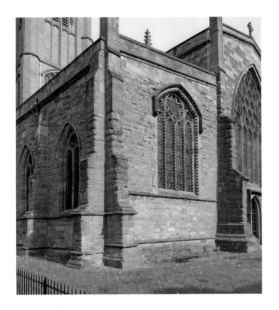

Top: the north aisle at Ludlow
Middle: the south aisle at Richard's Castle
Bottom: the polygonal chancel at Marden

this man was a different person from the mason who had worked at Leominster. Both masons, however, are likely to have worked at the cathedral before they subsequently moved on to other projects.

What is apparent from analysis of the works at Leominster, Weobley, Ledbury, Ludlow and Marden is that the closer these buildings are examined, the more difficult it becomes to say just how many masons were involved in their design. This is because, while the general effect of all the buildings is much the same, there are a host of differences between them in detail. When we turn to a second and quite separate set of buildings, a group of churches in the Wye valley to the west of Hereford, the problems of interpretation become far fewer. In these cases, the differences of detail are so slight as to leave little doubt that all the buildings are the work of a single mason, a highly idiosyncratic man whose style is distinctive enough to be instantly recognisable. The three churches are those of Madley, Eaton Bishop and Allensmore which, although different in size, character and appearance, have one important feature in common: they all make use of the same window moulding profile.[5] This, as we have seen, is a simple and immediately recognisable design found on the exterior jambs of all three churches, consisting of chamfers separated by a triangular recess made up of a right-angled isosceles triangle (*see p. 34*). The earliest of the three buildings on which this formation appears is the chancel at Madley, a remarkable structure with the unusual feature of a polygonal apse, to which a date of sometime after 1318 may be assigned (*see pp. 22–23*). The same profile is subsequently reproduced on the east windows of the nave and chancel at Eaton Bishop, and the nave windows at Allensmore. The mason's commitments at Madley appear to have drawn to a close by the early or mid-1320s, and he then moved to Eaton Bishop, a few miles to the east, where the glass in the new east window that he built can be dated to sometime after 1328. It may have been while he was at Eaton Bishop that he simultaneously carried out the refenestration at Allensmore, a village only a few miles further on again. His final commission, and one on which he appears to have been engaged for the rest of his working life, involved him returning to Madley, where in the 1330s he undertook the building of the magnificent Chilston aisle and the remodelling of the north aisle opposite it. The Chilston aisle is his masterpiece and shows him making use of the fully reticulated window tracery newly fashionable at that time: at Eaton Bishop and Allensmore he had used the familiar Herefordshire Y-shaped design (*see p. 14*). For all the distinctiveness – indeed, at times, the idiosyncrasy – of this man's work, it is clear that he must have received his initial training at the cathedral. The origins of both his mouldings profiles and his early patterns of window tracery can be traced to forms used in the cathedral workshop in the 1310s.

When we move onto the next generation of Decorated buildings, the direct links with the cathedral become both fewer and weaker. Other design sources come to the fore, among these Tewkesbury Abbey, where the eastern arm was being lavishly rebuilt by the Despensers, and a range of recently rebuilt churches in Herefordshire

Pembridge church, showing the detached tower and the west front with its reticulated windows

and south Shropshire, notably Ludlow and Weobley. The most substantial project begun in the county in the late 1320s was the rebuilding of the church at Pembridge, an ambitious undertaking which was to go on for some 15 years or more. The church is a big one, consisting of a nave with aisles and north porch, north and south transepts, a chancel and, unusually, a detached tower, of which there are seven examples in the county. The main source for most of Pembridge's stylistic motifs was the choir of Tewkesbury Abbey, where a novelty of the design was the use of wavy curve formations on all the mouldings of the presbytery arcade arches, the inner arches of the ambulatory and the exterior frames of the ambulatory chapel windows.[6] Wavy curves of precisely the same profile are found at Pembridge on the arcade arches, the chancel arch, the exterior frames of the big reticulated windows and the frames of the main doors. If the Pembridge mason was someone with a knowledge of regional architectural developments, however, he was almost certainly also someone who was locally based in Herefordshire. What points to this is the fact that most of his other stylistic borrowings are from churches very close to Pembridge, in Stretford hundred itself. Particularly strong are the links with the naves of Weobley and Kington, the south arcade of the nave at Lyonshall and the north aisle of the nave at

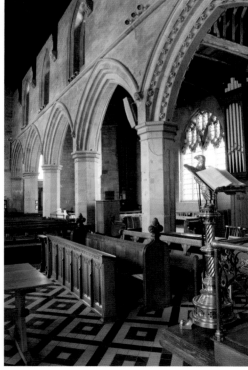

The closely related nave arcades at Pembridge (*left*) and Weobley (*right*)

Kinnersley, all of them churches within six or seven miles of the village. It is likely that the nave at Weobley, with its octagonal piers and moulded capitals, was the most immediate source for the design of the similar nave at Pembridge, and it is possible that there was some overlap in the labour forces for the two buildings. A lesser work probably to be associated with Pembridge is the north transept at Dilwyn, an addition to a mainly late thirteenth-century fabric, which has a number of features in common with its larger neighbour, among these the use of a half-arch between the nave aisle and the transept.

The north transept at Dilwyn

In the last group of Decorated churches, those dating from roughly the 1330s and the 1340s, it is possible to detect a wider range of influences, some of these from as far afield as the central Midlands. With one exception the churches are all in the north of the county or south Shropshire, three of them – Ludlow, Richard's Castle and Wigmore – being in this area, and the outlier, Kingsland, a little to the south-west in the Lugg valley.[7] Only at Kingsland was an end-to-end rebuilding attempted; elsewhere the works all took the form of piecemeal additions or alterations to existing fabrics. At Ludlow, in a renewal of the campaign which had opened with the reconstruction of the north aisle, the two transepts were remodelled; at Richard's Castle a transept was added on the north side and a new window inserted in the chancel east wall; and at Wigmore a transept was again added (this was later demolished). What distinguishes the work at all of these buildings is the use in them of curvilinear window tracery, a form which was quickly becoming fashionable in the east and south-east of the country and which now makes its appearance in the Welsh Marches. The east window of Richard's Castle is particularly fine, with its rich flowing tracery bending into a combination of mouchettes and cusped mandorla shapes over each pair of lights (*see p. 38*). The design sources for all the churches in the group point to possible links between them and some of the major building sites in the Midlands. The window at Richard's Castle is very close in design to one in Lichfield Cathedral, which likewise has two converging mouchettes and a cusped mandorla. The mouldings formations, however, invite comparison more with those at Gloucester Abbey, Worcester Cathedral and, further north, with the chancel of St Mary's, Warwick, and John of Gaunt's works at Kenilworth Castle. Since the works in Herefordshire almost certainly pre-date those at the latter two sites, it

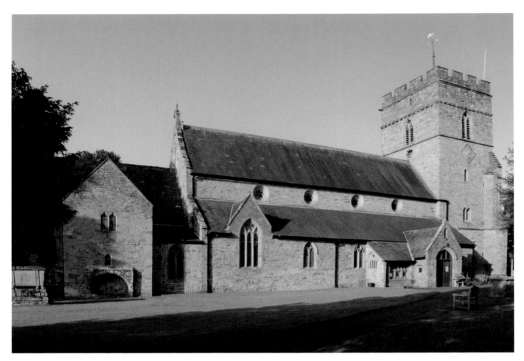

is likely that the Herefordshire masons, once their commitments in the county were over, went on to these bigger projects in the Midlands, taking their particular styles with them.

At Kingsland, which is very much the oddity in this late group, the design sources are quite different again. Kingsland is another sizeable building, with a tall west tower, an aisled nave with porch and attached chapel on the north side, a chancel and a vestry. There are details of the church's design, notably the tracery of the east window, which link it, as we have seen, with other buildings in the group, with sites in the Midlands, among these the choir of Lichfield. The most striking motifs, however, establish a connection with a quite different centre, St Augustine's Abbey, Bristol, now Bristol Cathedral. On both of the church's main doors – those in the porch and from the chancel to the vestry – a cusped three-sided polygonal head is used instead of a

Kingsland church from the south (*top*). The cusped head of the vestry doorway (*bottom*)

Almeley church as seen from the neighbouring castle mound to the south

conventional arch, a characteristic unique to the Bristol workshop, which used it on the tomb recesses in St Augustine's and on the main doorway at St Mary Redcliffe, close by. Almost certainly, the master mason responsible for Kingsland was someone who had received his initial training at Bristol. Below him, however, there were evidently other masons who brought with them experience from sites further north, in the Midlands, notably but not exclusively Lichfield Cathedral.

If these four groups of churches represent the work of all the most active and influential teams of masons in the county in the first half of the fourteenth century, there are nonetheless numerous other fabrics which were the object of varying degrees of attention in the same period, among them Stretton Grandison, which was completely rebuilt, Kingstone, Ashperton, Bodenham, Almeley, Stretford, Letton and Sarnesfield. In most of these cases it is likely that a minor local mason was responsible, a man perhaps who worked on no more than two or three churches all near to each other and who was otherwise engaged on more menial commissions. Just occasionally we can track the work of men of this sort in a locality. In the east of the county, for example, there was a mason or a group of masons, probably based in Ledbury, whose hallmark was the use of windows of three stepped lights rather like those in the chancel at Pembridge.[8] Examples of these men's work can be seen in the south chancel aisle at Ledbury and in the chancel at Ashperton. To the west of Hereford there was another freelance operator, who drew on motifs deriving from such sources as the thirteenth-century north transept of the cathedral, who was responsible for the nave at Dilwyn and possibly too the nave of Clehonger.[9] Yet another man again appears to have been responsible for the clerestory windows at Almeley and Lyonshall.[10] In southern Shropshire there was another man again who worked on the three churches of Chelmarsh (*see p. 30*), Kinlet and Stottesdon (all very close to one another), whose trademark, at least in big windows, was the use of a sexfoiled circle at the top instead of intersections.[11] Since all these craftsmen were usually operating well away from the main centres, their work often had a slightly idiosyncratic feel to it.

What is immediately apparent from any reconstruction of the history of church building in Herefordshire in the early fourteenth century is that there was little or no shortage of competent masons in the area at this time. It seems that no prospective patron who wished to undertake building work on a church would have encountered any difficulty in finding a contractor to meet his needs. Or if he happened not to know such a man personally, he would almost certainly have known someone who could put him in touch with one. It was the prolonged campaign at Hereford Cathedral, beginning in the 1290s and going on into the 1310s, which had first drawn these men into the county and then kept them there. As the years went by, and the

Tomb recesses in the south choir aisle of Hereford Cathedral, containing posthumous effigies of bishops

first arrivals either retired, moved on or succumbed to mortality, so numbers were maintained by the taking on of new staff. It was to these successive teams that prospective patrons would turn in the first instance if they were looking for a mason to undertake their project, particularly if it was a fairly substantial one. So long as building work at the cathedral was in progress, the likelihood is that any commissions of this sort would have been undertaken in the intervals between stages in the work there. Once the cathedral's operations were over, as they were by about 1320, the craftsmen would have been available more regularly for other employment.

The masons and tomb-making

If the cathedral's masons could take on the designing of churches as well as their actual construction, then those below them – the chisellers and sculptors – might likewise turn their hand to other types of activity. In an age when church building was essentially a seasonal activity and there were inevitable lulls between campaigns, these sorts of men might well find it useful to develop a sideline in the carving of funerary sculpture: that is to say, in the cutting of cross slab grave covers, incised slabs, effigial sculpture and the like. This was quite simply because the skills required of the mason were much the same as those looked for in the tomb sculptor. In each case, what was required was a reasonable competence in the cutting and chiselling of stone. The close connection between church building and funerary sculpture in Herefordshire in the Decorated period is highlighted by the wide popularity locally as tomb settings of low recesses cut into the wall, some of them decorated with ballflower. These low recesses are typically bonded into the wall, indicating that they were provided for when their immediate surroundings were built. The reason for their popularity may well have been the fact that they were used in the cathedral to accommodate the posthumous effigies of bishops commissioned by Bishop Swinfield for the choir aisles.

Some four- to five-dozen effigial tomb monuments have come down to us in Herefordshire from between 1280 and 1350, the heyday of Decorated architecture in the area. For a small county this is a not inconsiderable number. And it is worth remembering that it takes no account either of recorded losses from churches or of the large number of monuments that would once have existed in the friars' houses in the county, notably in Hereford itself. To the total for relief effigial monuments we have to add the huge number of incised slabs and cross slab grave covers which were commissioned locally in the same period, some of these of quite elaborate design. Cross slabs were almost certainly the most popular of all forms of commemoration in the central Marches in the thirteenth and fourteenth centuries, and they attracted a wide range of patrons, both clerical and lay. Good examples of the genre are found at Dilwyn, Aconbury, Brinsop, Richard's Castle and in Hereford Cathedral itself. Locally made slabs of thirteenth-century date, such as some of those at Aconbury, are often adorned by the decorative motif of a rosette.

Remains of cross slab grave covers at Dilwyn (*left*) and an effigy at Wolferlow to a lady of the Geneville family of Ludlow (*right*)

In some parts of the country for the medieval period it has proved possible to classify effigies stylistically so as to create series that can be connected with the work of a particular sculptor or school of sculptors. Unfortunately, it is not at all easy to do this in the case of Herefordshire, as the county's monuments vary so widely in style and design. In the whole corpus there are relatively few examples with enough motifs or mannerisms in common to suggest that they are all the work of the same hand. There is one useful test, however, which can be applied to produce an initial classification, and that is the petrological one of looking at the stone-type employed. The stone native to the county, which was drawn on in greatest quantity for church building and tomb sculpture in these years was the slightly grey, though sometimes pinkish, Old Red Sandstones, quarried at a number of sites in the county, notably at Capler in the parish of How Caple, on the Wye.[12] It was Capler stone, taken either by river or by road, which provided the building stone for much of the cathedral. Most thirteenth- and early fourteenth-century Herefordshire monuments of both effigial and non-effigial type are fashioned from this material. A few, however, found mainly in the east of the county, are not. These are of a high-quality limestone from the Painswick quarries in Gloucestershire. The tomb monuments in this stone would have been brought to the county most probably by water, first down the Severn and then up the Wye, being unloaded at either Ross-on-Wye or Hereford itself.

If we confine ourselves initially to looking at the three-dozen or so monuments that, on the evidence of the stone used, appear to be of local origin, then we immediately see that there is a group of just three that stand out for their superior quality. One is the figure of a priest in Mass vestments at Ledbury, dating from the late thirteenth century, and the others, the two excellent female effigies at Wolferlow (*see p. 46*) and Welsh Bicknor, carved perhaps a few years later. The identity of the Ledbury priest is unknown, but it is likely that the two female figures commemorate ladies of aristocratic birth: in the former case probably a lady of the Geneville family of Ludlow, and in the latter a lady of the de Huntleys, an important Marcher gentry family. All three figures are beautifully sculpted, a notable feature of the ladies being the sleek lines of their dresses as they fall to the ground. In each case, the lady's head is shown resting on a cushion supported by angels; and in each case too the long over-mantle is shown caught up, at Welsh Bicknor by being clasped in the lady's right hand and at Wolferlow by being draped over her left arm.[13] The handling of the drapery folds on the two figures is essentially alike, although at Welsh Bicknor the carving is shallower. Whether or not the figure of the priest and those of the two ladies are the work of the same sculptor is not clear. Stylistically, however, there is a third figure which can be linked with those of the ladies, the slightly later, hardly less accomplished figure of Precentor Swinfield (d.1311) in Hereford Cathedral, another elegant figure on which the folds fall almost symmetrically to the feet. In all four cases, it is natural to suppose the involvement of a cathedral-based mason.

Two other, quite different, effigies that appear to be from the same hand are the closely related figures of civilians at Woolhope and Upton Bishop. This pair are of greatly inferior quality to the effigies of the two ladies, and are the work of an altogether less accomplished sculptor. The monuments are both carved in low relief, and in each case the man is shown with crossed hands and clasping a book, under a trefoiled ogee canopy adorned with crockets, and, in the case of Upton Bishop, with ballflower. Both monuments can be dated to perhaps the 1320s or 1330s. In neither case do we know the identity of the man commemorated, but in each it is tempting to suspect an administrator or estate official, as both villages were held by ecclesiastical proprietors: Upton Bishop was held by the bishops, and Woolhope by the dean and chapter.

When we move beyond these two pairs of monuments to take in the other effigies in the county, it becomes more difficult to identify coherent stylistic groupings. The wider the range of figures, the vaguer become the similarities between them, and the

Hereford Cathedral: tomb effigy of Precentor John Swinfield

Upton Bishop church: tomb effigy of an unidentified civilian

Bodenham church: tomb effigy of a lady of the Devereux family and her young son

Left: Edvin Ralph church: tomb effigies of members of the de Edvin family

Above: Stretford church: tomb effigies of two members of the de la Bere family

Below: Foy church: small tomb effigy of an unknown civilian

more questionable the suggested degrees of affinity. It may be possible, however, to posit a few more connections between some of the county's numerous, and reasonably distinctive, female effigies. A couple of figures that appear to belong together are the similar-looking pair at Ewyas Harold to Clarissa de la Warr (née Tregoz) (d.1270) and Bodenham to a Devereux lady and her young son. Both figures are more than competently sculpted, with the details well handled. In each case, however, the drapery folds are heavier than at Wolferlow and Welsh Bicknor, and the lines less sleek, pointing to the hand of a different sculptor. It is hard to say whether the knight and lady and pair of ladies at Edvin Ralph should also be included with this group (see p. 49). These figures are all fairly simply conceived, with little or no sophistication, and in the case of the ladies the drapery folds fall in straight lines to the ground. It is possible that these are by a different hand again.

As we have seen with the Woolhope and Upton Bishop effigies, a notable feature of some of the county's effigial monuments is that they are carved in fairly low relief from sandstone blocks of distinctly shallow depth. This is a noticeable feature too of some of the largely uniform posthumous monuments of bishops commissioned by Bishop Swinfield to line the choir aisles of the cathedral. In particular, the two figures attributed to Bishops de Mapenore and de Vere stand out as quite obviously less boldly sculpted than all the others (see p. 44). Pevsner, commenting on this aspect, wondered if it might be indicative of their earlier date, while another writer has suggested that it might represent a deliberate attempt to simulate antique carving.[14] In the light of the shallow-relief character of some of the other effigies in the county, however, it is possible to suggest a different explanation: namely, that the Herefordshire stone could not always be quarried in blocks deep enough to carry figure carving, and that the sculptors were accordingly limited in what they could achieve. Two other groups of effigies in the county exhibit this same quality of relative flatness. In the north of the county are the two curious-looking pairs of effigies at Stretford commemorating members of the de la Bere family, probably Sir Robert de la Bere and his wife and their son, Sir John, and his wife, Agnes (see p. 49). Both pairs of figures date from some 30 years later than those at the cathedral, and are clearly the product of different sculptors. The second, sharply contrasting, group of effigies consists of three figures, two in the far south of the county at Foy (see p. 49) and Llangarron, and the third over the county border at Trellech (Mon.).[15] All three figures are crudely carved and undersized, those at Foy and Llangarron showing civilians, and that at Trellech a lady. In the case of the Llangarron figure both hands are shown folded low on the lap, while at Trellech and Foy just one hand is shown on the lap and the other raised and apparently holding an object. At Foy the man is shown somewhat incongruously standing on a rounded object. All three figures appear to be the products of a Welsh-born sculptor, probably someone based in the Monmouth area. What they and the pairs of effigies at Stretford have in common, however, is that they are cut from Old Red Sandstone. As with the effigies at the cathedral, the explanation for their shallowness is very likely again the correspondingly shallow seams from which they were cut.

If the county's locally produced effigies form a rather amorphous group, lacking in distinctiveness and hard to classify, quite the opposite may be said of those effigial monuments which were imported – that is to say, carved elsewhere and brought into the county or produced on site from imported stone blocks. These include some of the most impressive of all effigial monuments of their date anywhere in England. Consideration of the origins and characteristics of this remarkable group takes us by a roundabout route back to the business of church building in the Decorated period.

By far the grandest and most celebrated of the 'imported' monuments is that at Much Marcle, commemorating Blanche Mortimer, Lady Grandison (d.1347), a work of the highest distinction. It is made of fine-grained oolitic limestone from the Painswick quarries in Gloucestershire. Lady Grandison is shown at rest lying on a richly panelled chest, with her hands on her waist, her right hand placed flat and her left clutching a rosary, and the bottom of her dress falling naturalistically over the edge of the tomb and down most of its depth. Behind the effigy is a fine back-panel with niches, and above it, first, double coving carved in imitation of a vault and then, above this, a canopy crowned with cusping. A monument comparable to that at Marcle is the now mutilated ensemble in the north-east chapel at Ledbury to a Pauncefot lady, a composition once of similar structure and on which the train of the gown is again shown tumbling naturalistically down the side.[16] While the monument is probably not by the same sculptor as Lady Grandison's commission, it is almost certainly by one of that sculptor's assistants or apprentices.

Top: Much Marcle church: tomb monument of Blanche, Lady Grandison. *Bottom*: Ledbury church: tomb monument of a lady of the Pauncefot family

There are strong grounds for believing that Lady Grandison's monument was the work of a mason-sculptor who had been trained at Exeter and was employed on carving the image screen on the west front of the cathedral there.[17] The bishop of Exeter from 1327 to 1369 was John de Grandison, younger brother of Peter, Lord Grandison, Lady Blanche's husband, a highly conscientious diocesan and a keen patron of the arts and architecture. Shortly before the Black Death Grandison embarked on building the image screen, in which his own miniature burial chapel was to be incorporated, and the figure sculpture on it affords the closest stylistic parallels to the Much Marcle effigy.[18] Work on the screen appears to have come to a halt in 1348, almost certainly as a result of the plague, and one of the team of sculptors, perhaps the leader, it seems, was brought to Herefordshire by the bishop's brother, Blanche's husband, to take on the commission for her tomb. Peter himself was to die barely a decade later, and his own tomb monument of the 1350s, in the Lady Chapel of Hereford Cathedral and another ambitious composition, is almost certainly by the same sculptor. Three other monuments in the Marches identifiable as the work of the same master are those at Clehonger to Sir Richard de Pembridge (d.c.1346) and at Abergavenny Priory to Lawrence Hastings, earl of Pembroke (d.1348), and his half-brother, Sir William (d.1349), both again of Painswick stone. A possible fourth is the monument of Sir John de Freyne (d.c.1340) at Moccas. The signature feature of this craftsman's treatment of his male figures, although less so of his female, is the restless poses that he invests them with. At Clehonger Sir Richard de Pembridge is shown twisting over sideways, his head turned in one direction and the lower part of his body in the other, in the manner of an action effigy (see p. 53). Whether or not the mason-sculptor ever returned to work at Exeter is not known. All that can be said for certain is that he disappears from the scene in Herefordshire sometime before the end of the 1350s. He may have died in that decade. What is interesting about his career is that he should have made the transition from façade sculpture to tomb sculpture, a move of a kind similar to that made a generation earlier, in all probability, by some of the original mason-sculptors employed at Hereford Cathedral.

If work at Exeter was brought to a halt in 1348 by the plague, likewise in Herefordshire the appalling mortality wrought havoc with the related trades of building and figure-sculpture. Progress on the eastern arm of the cathedral had already slowed by 1320 because of a shortage of money, and the sweeping away of much of the labour force eliminated any prospect of early renewal. Operations on the incomplete south-east transept and the proposed new chapter house were not to be resumed until the early 1360s.[19] At the same time, it seems that there was a parallel collapse in the funerary sculpture trade across the county. The long series of locally produced effigial monuments draws to a close in the late 1340s with the

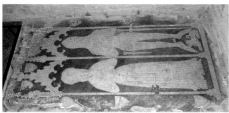

Top left: Clehonger church: tomb effigy of Sir Richard de Pembridge
Above left: Allensmore church: tomb slab of Sir Andrew Herley and his wife
Above right: Pembridge church: tomb monument of Nicholas Gour and his wife

two shallow-relief pairs of effigies at Stretford, which may be dated to no later than 1350. The few freestone effigial monuments that have come down to us from around Hereford from the second half of the century, appear to have been produced in or near quarries outside the county, notably the Painswick quarries in Gloucestershire.

The two finest monuments in the county in this later Painswick series are the two pairs of effigies at Pembridge to Nicholas and John Gour and their respective wives (*c*.1370–80). In addition to the monuments in freestone, there is one of alabaster, that commemorating Sir Richard Pembridge (d.1375) in Hereford Cathedral. It is much harder to say what happened to the production locally of cross slab grave covers in the second half of the century, because the great majority are almost impossible to date with any precision. However, insofar as any conclusions can be reached on the basis of stylistic analysis, it seems likely that again there was a breakdown around the time of the Black Death, with production slowing to a trickle thereafter.

It seems a reasonable assumption that many of the mason-sculptors who had been responsible for producing these different types of monument had been swept away in the general mortality.

What eventually was to take the place of these earlier monuments was a type which had not been seen in the county before, a product which was to become something of a local speciality: the incised and colour-filled inlay slab. In design these monuments closely resemble some of the grander brasses of the day, but instead of using brass inlays for the figures, inscription and architectural surrounds they drew on a white, probably calcium-based, inlay, on which the design was then incised and the colour applied. Most of the surviving examples are grand effigial compositions, with big figures of priests or laymen and their wives, usually shown under canopies, and with an inscription surrounding the whole. Excellent examples of the genre are to be found at Canon Pyon, Dilwyn, Allensmore and in Hereford Cathedral. The fine slab at Allensmore commemorating Sir Andrew Herley (d.1392) and his wife survives in especially good condition (*see p. 53*).[20] Inlay slabs enjoyed a wide popularity with the better-off sort of clients for some 30 or 40 years, but their production appears to have ceased in around 1400. After that, there is little evidence of any local production of monuments in the county at all.

The fates of the building and funerary sculpture trades in Herefordshire thus appear to have been closely related. The two rose and fell together. At times when there was a boom in church building in the county, a class of mason-sculptors was called into being, who could turn their hand to the production of tomb sculpture when needed. When there was a collapse in church building, as there was after the Black Death and the fall in population that followed, the production of tomb sculpture was likewise halted. In the century or so from 1348 not only was the supply of skilled labour no longer available; the level of building activity which had sustained it for so long was also gone. In Herefordshire and south Shropshire there was to be very little church building in the fifteenth and early sixteenth centuries. Perpendicular architecture is but rarely encountered in churches in the two counties except, notably, at St Laurence's, Ludlow. Precisely why there was not a pick-up in church building when the population eventually recovered towards the end of the fifteenth century is a question to which we will return.

3

The Claims of Piety

ALTHOUGH IT IS probably Herefordshire and the central Marches which saw the most intense church building in the Decorated period, there were certain other parts of the country where the level of building activity was still high. Areas that stand out are Lincolnshire, Oxfordshire and the Thames valley, Kent and the south-east of Yorkshire. Just as in earlier centuries, a good deal of work was undertaken on the greater churches – the cathedrals, abbeys and richer priories. Exeter Cathedral was almost completely rebuilt from 1275, and there was extensive remodelling at York Minster and the cathedrals of Wells, Ely, Lichfield and Hereford. It was not so much on the cathedrals, however, that the Decorated style was to have its greatest impact; it was rather on the parish churches. At the parochial level there was much piece-meal reconstruction and enlargement, with typically an aisle added here or a side chapel there, and relatively few churches escaping attention altogether. There were even a few complete rebuildings. In south Lincolnshire the magnificent churches of Grantham and Boston are almost entirely works of the Decorated period. In those parts of the country where building activity was at a low ebb, it was usually because adverse circumstances stood in the way. In the far north, hostilities with the Scots led to a collapse in building in Northumberland, while in Hampshire and Sussex heavy rain and coastal flooding took their inevitable toll. Across the country as a whole, however, the level of construction activity seems to have been impressive. Why was this? And why, in particular, was there so much activity in Herefordshire?

Church building and chantries

The process, usually piecemeal, of rebuilding and repairing church fabrics was one that extended right across the Middle Ages and can be explained in a variety of ways. In the aftermath of the Conquest one very important factor was the steady rise in population. In the late Saxon period most English parish churches had been built as simple two-cell structures, composed of a tiny chancel and nave, and an arched opening connecting the two. Between the late eleventh and the early four-teenth centuries, however, as the population expanded and more space was needed, so it became necessary to enlarge these buildings. Typically, the nave would be extended to the west and an aisle added to one side. Later, as architectural fashions changed and the Romanesque style gave way to Gothic, a second factor was found in the need to keep fabrics up to date. Small, old fashioned-looking structures would be replaced by grander, more stylish ones. The nave arcade might be remodelled, the roof replaced or new fittings provided. Quite commonly, in the later thirteenth century, as building technologies advanced, the tiny, round-headed windows of old would be replaced by big traceried openings, allowing for lighter interiors and ena-bling the stained glass painters to show off their talents.

In the last century before the Reformation another factor that made for rebuild-ing was the intense competition between parishes, which led to rivalry between them in the size and splendour of their churches. In the West Country, and espe-cially in Somerset, parishes can be seen vying with one another in the sheer loftiness of their towers. Nor was regular church building and refurbishment ever solely the result of the secular motives of local pride and changing fashion. Changes in litur-gical doctrine and practice played their part too. In the wake of the Fourth Lateran Council of 1215, when a new emphasis was placed on the miraculous element in the Mass – the transformation of the bread and wine into the body and blood of Christ – it was increasingly felt that chancels should be opulent enough to provide appro-priate settings for this central act of Christian worship. In the years after 1250 many magnificent new chancels were constructed, each of them creating an image of the heavenly Jerusalem on earth.

All of these considerations – and others besides – help to explain why there was such intense church building in England in the late Middle Ages. Yet there was another factor again, and one of a more specific nature, which helps to account for the boom of the Decorated years in particular. This was a major change that occurred towards the end of the thirteenth century in the way that post obit inter-cession for the soul was organised. For the first time it became possible for middling and lesser proprietors to arrange personalised prayers for their souls and those of friends and relatives named by them. It was this opening up of intercession to a much wider patron class which, more than anything else, led to so many piecemeal additions to church fabrics in the Decorated period.

The instinct to make some sort of intercessory provision for the soul, however modest, was one that sprang naturally to the Christian mind. The official teaching of the Church was that the souls of the deceased were tried and tested in purgatory, and that the length of the period of pain could be shortened by the prayers of the living faithful. The more generous the provision made for prayer, it was believed, the greater the chance that the trials of the soul would be curtailed.

Down to the thirteenth century the provision of *post obit* intercession had been largely a monopoly of those great institutional power-houses of prayer, the monasteries. The main function of all monastic institutions in the Middle Ages was to act as communities of remembrance in which the souls of deceased founders, benefactors and brethren could be prayed for regularly on the anniversaries of their deaths. By the early or mid twelfth century, however, in many of the larger houses the numbers of those whose passage in the afterlife had to be taken care of in this way were becoming so great that the entire system was in danger of breakdown. At Durham, in the massive Liber Vitae which lay on the cathedral's high altar, the names of no fewer than 3,150 men and women were inscribed, for whose souls intercession had to be offered on a regular basis.[1] If the monks were not to find themselves turning away potential benefactors, a way had to be found of reconciling growing demand with the intercessory workload placed on individual brethren.

One innovation which proved a help was for the benefactor to nominate and pay for a member of the house to offer intercession exclusively on his behalf. In 1216, for example, a Bedfordshire gentleman, Reginald de Baa, made a grant of lands in Eaton Socon to Bushmead priory, to maintain a chaplain charged specifically with praying for the souls of de Baa himself and those named by him. A few years earlier Geoffrey, count of Brittany, had gone much further in making a specific request for daily masses to be said in Rouen Cathedral in perpetuity for the soul of his deceased brother Henry, the Young King.[2] It is in the establishment of these sorts of arrangements, in which bespoke provision was made for the offering of intercession, that the origins of the later perpetual chantries are to be found. Over time, what had originated as a way of easing the pressure on a burdened monastic community was appreciated by prospective patrons as a way of instituting arrangements of a similar sort in churches that were not monastic – that is, in colleges, chapels, castle oratories, but most of all in local parish churches. Uninterrupted intercession for the soul, hitherto a service provided almost exclusively by the monastic Orders, could now be obtained by other means.

This was a development of importance especially to members of the middling country landowner class – the knights and well-to-do esquires – because at precisely this time other changes independently were inclining them to take a closer interest in the parish church placed by the family manor-house. In part as a result of Henry II's legal reforms, which made the shire and not the feudal honor the key unit of local government, the ties between the knightly class and the old feudal honors, from which they held their lands, were weakening; and with this weakening went a loosening too of their ties with the honorial monasteries in which their fore-bears had generally been buried. By the thirteenth century the knightly landowners were coming to see themselves as a territorial rather than a strictly feudal elite, office-holders in shire and hundred and spokesmen for their shires in parliament. As a result, they increasingly directed their religious patronage to the local parish church; and by the fourteenth century it was typically in the parish church that they were buried. When, towards the end of their days, they came to make arrangements for burial and funerary obsequies, typically they made intercessory provision at the same time. By the fourteenth century, when the intercessory system was fully devel-oped, there was a sliding scale of such provision ranging from yearly anniversary masses at one end to full-scale perpetual chantries at the other. Well-to-do gentry and townsmen could typically afford to go for a full perpetual chantry. Conceived at its most modest, a chantry might take the form of little more than a side altar in an existing aisle and the provision of a landed endowment to go with it. On a much grander scale, however, it might involve the construction of a purpose-built chapel to accommodate the altar and the endowment to support several chaplains.

It is possible to calculate roughly how many perpetual chantries were established in the late medieval period by sifting through the licences for alienation of land to the Church recorded on the royal chancery rolls. From 1279 it was obligatory for anyone intending to transfer land held from the king to endow a chantry to obtain such a licence and pay a fee for it. In the first 20 years of the licensing system numbers grew fairly slowly, a mere 36 being issued in the period to the end of the century. In the course of the next half-century, however, there was an explosion in numbers, with no fewer than 934 being issued between 1299 and 1349. After 1349 numbers fell back, with some 670 issued between 1349 and 1399, and only 290 in the half-century after that.[3]

What is apparent from these figures is that the period of the greatest popular-ity of chantries coincided with the heyday of the Decorated style of architecture. The boom in chantry provision was thus bound to have an effect on the design and construction of churches, and on the ways in which space was arranged and used within them. What happened was that previously simple two-cell churches were progressively adapted and enlarged to create additional altar space, resulting in the development of more irregular ground plans, the fragmentation of space internally, and the appropriation of whole areas for burial chapels for the well-to-do.

In Herefordshire and the Marches, the need for such additional space was all the greater because, insofar as surviving fabrics afford any guide, building work appears to have been on only a limited scale in the thirteenth century. Most of Herefordshire's churches were of twelfth-century date and took the form of small aisleless struc-tures, of the kind that can still be seen at Kilpeck, Moccas and Pipe Aston. Typically,

Dilwyn church from the north-west, showing the north transept and aisle

Westhide church from the south-west, showing the south chapel and stocky, west tower

additions to these structures in the Decorated period took the form of transeptal chapels built at right angles to the main fabric so as to form an area in which an altar could be placed and burial space created, with a parclose screen separating it from the rest of the church. Examples of such projecting chapels are legion in the county. Chapels built out from the north side of the fabric are found at Clehonger, Dilwyn and Richard's Castle, and similar ones on the side opposite at Letton and King's Pyon. At Westhide the chapel was built on the south side of the nave and an arcade cut in the wall so as to form an aisle parallel with the old fabric. In some cases, as at Clehonger, the founder's tomb was sited at the entrance to the chapel, in order to attract the attention of worshippers (*see p. 53*). More often, however, as at King's Pyon and Letton, it was placed in a low recess in the end wall. Where two or more chantries were founded in a church, as for example at Bishopstone or Kinlet (Salop), a projecting chapel would be built on each side, in this way creating a cross plan. If, as was often the case, economy enforced the location of the new altar in an existing aisle, then attention might be drawn to the setting architecturally by a rise in the roofline and the insertion of a new window.[4]

Hereford's own saint: the cult of Thomas de Cantilupe

While the explosion in chantry provision goes a long way to explaining why such a volume of building work was undertaken at parish church level in the fourteenth century, there is a second and very different reason which helps to account for the upsurge in activity in Herefordshire specifically. This is a phenomenon unique to the religious life of the border area: the mood of renewed spirituality associated with the cult of the diocese's local saint and Hereford's former bishop, St Thomas de Cantilupe.

Cantilupe's career, spent mainly in the universities, had little in it to suggest the strength of the cult that would be associated with his name after his death. While he was an upright and conscientious man, renowned for his personal probity, he did not exude the saintliness of a Becket; nor did he make a particular virtue of austerity and sacrifice. He appears nonetheless to have been a forceful, even a charismatic figure, and he inspired deep devotion in those who were close to him.

Cantilupe was a scion of an ancient aristocratic family with extensive lands in the Midlands and southern Marches.[5] His father William was the son of King John's steward, and his mother Millicent the daughter of a great Norman lord. His elder brother William married a co-heiress of the de Braose family and through her acquired the Marcher lordship of Abergavenny. Although as a child Thomas had once expressed an ambition to be a soldier, he was destined like his brother Hugh for a career in the Church; and for this he prepared with a lengthy programme of study. According to Robert of Gloucester, his friend and later his secretary, he was despatched by his family to Paris, then Europe's leading university, where he was to follow the Arts course for some five or six years. In 1245 he was present at the Council of Lyons, where he was appointed a chaplain by none other than Pope Innocent iv. Around this time, having by now graduated in the Arts, he embarked on a second programme of study, the arduous course of training that would prepare him for a career in ecclesiastical administration. Enrolling at Orléans to begin the study of Roman or civil law, in around 1252 he went back to Paris to complement this with the study of canon law, the law of the Church. In 1255 he returned to England, to complete his legal studies at Oxford, and in 1261 he was elected chancellor of the university there.

By this time the political storm clouds were gathering in England, and there was a worsening of relations between the king, Henry iii, and his hard-line baronial opponents, among whom Simon de Montfort was the most prominent. Cantilupe's views on the growing crisis owed much to the influence of his uncle, Walter de Cantilupe, bishop of Worcester, a leading baronial supporter, and he followed his kinsman in inclining to the baronial side. In 1263 he was appointed one of the baronial representatives at the judgement given on the dispute by King Louis of France at Amiens in 1264, and in the following year he was made Chancellor of England. After de Montfort's defeat and death at the Battle of Evesham, and the consequent reassertion of royal authority, he tactfully retired to Paris. In 1275 he was elevated to the see of Hereford through the good offices of his predecessor, John le Breton, whose favour he enjoyed. He was to prove an active diocesan, throwing himself into local administration, perambulating his see, conducting visitations and, according to one report, regularly preaching to his flock through an interpreter. After about 1280, however, he was to find himself increasingly embroiled in a bitter jurisdictional dispute with John Pecham, the tetchy archbishop of Canterbury. In 1282 he decided to take his case on appeal to the pope in Italy, and it was while he was awaiting judgement there that on 25 August he died.

The response in the diocese to Cantilupe's sudden and unexpected death was quite remarkable. His remains were brought back to his cathedral and interred in the Lady Chapel, and miracles were soon reported. In 1287 a magnificent new shrine-like tomb monument was constructed in the north transept, which was closer to the main entrance, and the bishop's miraculous powers were soon fully revealed. For a brief period Cantilupe's cult was the most popular in England. Between 1287 and 1312 over 400 miracles were credited to him, a figure surpassed in the records of medieval England only by the 700 miracles attributed to Becket.[6]

This extraordinary turn of events could hardly have been more welcome to the chapter of Hereford Cathedral. For a long time, the dean and canons had felt the want of a big, prestigious shrine in their church. At the turn of the twelfth and thirteenth centuries attempts had been made to kick-start the cult of St Ethelbert, the East Anglian king whose bones they possessed, but the campaign had enjoyed little success. The presence of the remains of a popular local saint conferred rank and status on a cathedral. Durham had the bones of St Cuthbert, Lichfield those of St Chad, Winchester of St Swithun, Worcester of Sts Oswald and Wulfstan, and Canterbury of course Becket. Hereford was one of the few English cathedrals to lack a distinguished saint whose remains were the object of widespread popular veneration. Once Thomas de Cantilupe's healing powers had been revealed, Richard Swinfield, his successor in the see and his one-time chaplain, immediately seized the opportunity to promote his predecessor's cult. The process of canonisation which he initiated and to which he devoted the greater part of his episcopate, however, was to prove agonisingly slow.[7] Not until 1307 were official local enquiries

Top: Hereford Cathedral: the shrine of St Thomas de Cantilupe (1287; refurbished 2008)
Middle: detail of the shrine (north side). *Bottom*: detail of the shrine (south side)

into Cantilupe's reputation set in motion, and even after these had drawn to a close there were lengthy delays at the curia. Fresh letters of petition and further lobbying by the king and bishops were both needed to keep the process on track. It was not until April 1320 that the holy grail of canonisation was finally achieved, and by that time Swinfield himself was dead. Indeed, the local flowering of the cult was already well past its peak. Nonetheless, indulgences were still regularly issued by bishops to would-be pilgrims to encourage them to visit the shrine.

So long as it lasted, the cult of St Thomas was to be the agent for a major spiritual regeneration in the diocese of Hereford. A measure of the saint's popularity is to be found in the level of pilgrim offerings made at his shrine. As early as 1290–91, not long after the translation of his remains to the north transept, the sum of no less than £178 10s 7d was accounted for, pointing to the annual passage of some thousands of visitors.[8] In just one year – 1287 – no fewer than 160 miracles were reported at the shrine.[9] These are figures that more than matched those achieved at the shrine of St Thomas of Canterbury at this time.

The enormous popular interest in the cult and the pilgrim traffic it attracted both had significant local repercussions. Interest in the bishop's healing powers was to be found at all levels of society in the diocese. Especially noteworthy was the following among the local nobility and gentry, the people, in many cases holders of advowsons, who were often responsible for church building. In 1290 Sir Roger Mortimer of Chirk (Denbighshire), for example, a junior member of the family based at Wigmore, was to be numbered among the beneficiaries of the saint's healing abilities. When one day the knight was riding near London, a falcon of his was hit by a stone which shattered its eye, and its owner, recalling the saint's past interventions in favour of birds, bent a penny over it, and the creature was revived.[10] On the Mortimer family's estates in Herefordshire and the Marches a significant number of their tenantry were likewise to benefit from the saint's interventions. Among such were three villagers from Kingsland, near Leominster, one of whom, John, was cured of a paralysis which had afflicted him for five years, and the other two, Margery and Christina, women who were relieved of a crippling disability.[11] The Mortimers themselves were actually by no means in the forefront of devotion to the cult, as their family and the Cantilupes had been on opposite sides in the baronial wars of the 1260s. It is tempting, however, to suspect a connection between the heightened religious sensibility evident at this time and the family's activity as church builders between 1290 and 1340, the period of the cult's heyday. The family were involved in activity well beyond that immediately occasioned by the need to ensure the salvation of their own souls.

Among the greater gentry of the county there was at least one knight who had benefited from the saint's intercession, and that was Sir Miles Pychard, lord of Almeley and Letton, several times parliamentary knight of the shire for Herefordshire and a future sheriff of the county. For nearly a decade Sir Miles had been living with the effects of severe injuries he had sustained in a tournament. At Bishop Swinfield's suggestion, however, in 1287 he had attended the saint's translation, making the journey by cart, and he was healed at the shrine on Easter Sunday, 6 April.[12] Again, it is tempting to suspect a connection between the miraculous happening and the family's later church building activities, in their case at Almeley, which was substantially rebuilt at the turn of the thirteenth and fourteenth centuries (*see p. 43*). There can be little doubting lordly responsibility for the work here, as the church stood cheek-by-jowl with the castle or manor house, and the family held the advowson, the right of presenting the incumbent.

A second important local knight who could attest the saint's healing capacity was Sir John de Havering, lord of Vowchurch and a knight in Edmund of Cornwall's army in Wales in 1287. Havering had sent a deaf boy serving in his retinue to Hereford in the hope of receiving a cure, and the lad was to return fully healed. Several years later, the same knight was to witness a second miracle, this time the revival of a boy who had fallen from Conwy bridge onto the rocks below and whose body was made whole.[13] Sometime in the early fourteenth century a member of the de Havering family was almost certainly a part-contributor to the cost of rebuilding the church at Vowchurch.[14] If the connection between gratitude to the saint and personal piety as indicated by church building is only occasionally as clear or direct as it is in these few cases, it is nonetheless worth recalling that the boom in church building in the diocese of Hereford coincided precisely with the years of the cult's greatest popularity. And it is equally fair to make the reverse point: that, as the cult fell into decline, so too did the level of church building. Devotion to the cult of St Thomas de Cantilupe ran deep in

Credenhill church: stained glass window depicting Thomas Becket and Thomas de Cantilupe (*right*)

Herefordshire landed society. To knights such as Roger Mortimer, Miles Pychard and John de Havering, Cantilupe was a social equal: a Marcher lord descended from an Anglo-Norman lineage who held land as a tenant-in-chief and was the commander of an armed retinue. Throughout this period there were close ties between the county's knightly elite and the clerical community of Cantilupe's cathedral at Hereford. At one time or another, members of the Charlton, Pembridge, Talbot, Chandos, Havering, Dunre and de la Bere families were all to be found in the chapter's ranks.[15] For virtually the whole of his episcopate Bishop Swinfield was to have a member of the Mortimer family serving as his steward.[16] Cantilupe's saintly image was to feature in the stained glass windows with which these people adorned their churches and chapels. In Credenhill church the saint was to appear alongside Thomas Becket in a window almost certainly paid for by the Talbot family, and which survives today.

If Cantilupe's cult was to prove the unexpected means to a major spiritual renewal in Herefordshire and the central Marches, it might yet have had relatively little effect on church building had it not been for one thing more: namely, the availability locally of a major supply of masons and other skilled craftsmen who could take on all the work. Church building – at least church building on any scale – required the services of many types of skilled craftsmen: masons who could draw up working designs, order materials and supervise construction; carpenters who could construct the timber roofs; painters who could decorate the walls with paintings illustrating biblical or moralising themes; and stained glass artists who could glaze the windows. Men with these sorts of skills were usually to be found in the Middle Ages at major construction sites such as those associated with cathedrals, abbeys and castles or manor-houses. In Herefordshire around 1300 much the most important such site was Hereford Cathedral itself. As we have seen, the pilgrim flow to St Thomas's shrine was such that it paid for an extensive programme of remodelling which embraced not only the two big towers but also the eastern transepts and the aisles of both the choir and nave. It was the teams of skilled masons who had worked on the cathedral who, between building campaigns and after all the work was finished, went on to transform the diocese's parish churches.

The rebuilding of the cathedral was to have a far greater effect on church building in its vicinity than some of the other big rebuilding projects of the late Middle Ages did on their hinterlands. The great remodelling of Winchester Cathedral, for example, undertaken between the 1360s and the 1440s, had little or no effect in administering a kick-start to church building in Hampshire and surrounding counties in the same period. This was principally because there was neither much interest in church building locally at the time nor the money to pay for such work if there had been. A century earlier, the equally ambitious end-to-end remodelling of

Exeter Cathedral from 1260 to 1360 had but a limited effect in stimulating church building in the West Country in the years that it was going on. The big rebuilding of parish churches in the three south-western counties was to come much later, in the fifteenth century, when the wealth from the cloth trade was to pay for it.

In Herefordshire and south Shropshire the relationship between the cathedral and the diocese was to prove strikingly different from that found in these other cases. The rebuilding programme at the cathedral was to feed quite directly into a wider movement of local church maintenance and renewal. Not only did the masons who had worked at the cathedral go on to work on several dozen churches in the surrounding areas; they carried with them the rich repertory of motifs and stylistic mannerisms which they had developed in their long years of work at the cathedral. The result was a broad continuum of building activity between the mother church and the many lesser churches dependent on it. In this respect a parallel is to be drawn with the experience of the mid twelfth century, when the talented teams of sculptors who had worked on the capitals and other decorative details in the cathedral moved out to sculpt similar features in Herefordshire's parish churches, taking with them the lavish repertory of motifs which they had developed.[17] Elsewhere in England, in the Decorated period, a possible analogy is to be drawn with the position in Lincolnshire, where the masons who had worked on the tower and the eastern arm of Lincoln Cathedral went on to work on the liturgical furnishings in some of the county's many parish churches.

What lay behind the remarkable surge in church building in Herefordshire in the fourteenth century was, therefore, in part the mood of religious enthusiasm which we have seen was associated with the cult of the diocese's local saint, Thomas de Cantilupe. More specifically, however, it was the result of the sheer number of perpetual chantry foundations brought into being in this period. If the Cantilupe cult was responsible for stimulating an interest in church building generally, it was the wave of chantry foundations which explains why side aisles and transept chapels figure so prominently among the projects undertaken.

4

The Clergy as Builders

THE BUILDING OR rebuilding of churches in medieval England was a creative enterprise which turned on a collaboration between two groups of people – on the one hand, the client or clients commissioning the work and, on the other, the masons and other specialist craftsmen employed to make a reality of it. The mason's task was principally to draw up a possible design, assemble and supervise the labour force and oversee construction. The responsibility of the client, for his part, was to lay down the specifications for the commission, indicate the size of the budget available, prescribe what stones or other materials were to be used, and provide advice, where this was needed, on points of detail. Where the project to be undertaken was a fairly unambitious one, the role of the client would have been largely passive, the architectural vision for the project being formulated by the master mason in charge. Where the project was a larger one, however, the client's role would have been more dynamic, involving a creative partnership with the mason and craftsmen to formulate ideas on such matters as design and decoration, furnishing and sightlines. Typically, the terms on which clients secured the services of their specialist contractors were set down in a contract, a document which in most cases took the form of an indenture. Such agreements would usually specify such details as the task or commission to be undertaken, the level of reward to be offered, the materials which each party was to supply and the time allowed for completion. Well over 100 contracts have come down to us from medieval England, for a variety of building commissions – for churches, manor houses, colleges and urban tenement buildings. Unfortunately, however, not one example has survived relating to a church in the diocese of Hereford.

To understand the social and religious context for the boom in church building in the central March in the fourteenth century, therefore, we need to look in some detail at the clients or patrons responsible for initiating these projects, considering the means available to them, the social or kinship ties that held them together, the kinds of projects for which they were responsible, and the influences to which they were subject when exercising their patronage. These are matters which take us somewhat away from a consideration of architecture as such into an exploration of lay and ecclesiastical society in the fourteenth-century diocese and the economic foundations underpinning it. Although Herefordshire and south Shropshire may be considered today a somewhat remote part of the world, in the age of Swinfield and his successors it was one by no means detached from the wider social and religious currents of the age. On the contrary, in some respects, as we have seen, it stood at the very forefront of contemporary movements of popular religious belief.

Chancels

Since at least the 1220s there had been conventions, to a greater or lesser degree formally accepted, which determined the matter of responsibility for the maintenance and repair of church fabrics. Broadly speaking, it was agreed that the rector should take on responsibility for maintaining the chancel, while the lay congregation assumed a like responsibility for the fabric west of the chancel arch: that is to say, the nave, porch and tower.[1] Where a church had been appropriated – in other words, its revenues assigned in part to support a monastery – and the rector was, in consequence, a corporate religious body, this might result in the construction of a large and opulent chancel, to provide an appropriately magnificent setting for celebration of the Mass. All too often, however, corporate rectors were found neglecting their responsibilities and, especially where there was a resident lord of the manor, it was the laity's part of the fabric that was architecturally the more showy.

In Herefordshire and Shropshire in the early fourteenth century there were indeed some quite splendid chancel rebuildings undertaken by monasteries. Two of the most impressive examples are found in south Shropshire at Stottesdon and Shifnal, each a church in the ownership of Shrewsbury Abbey, and the former almost certainly rebuilt shortly after the convent's appropriation of the benefice in 1283.[2] In Herefordshire itself, the Dean and Chapter of Hereford Cathedral were responsible for one outstanding rebuilding, that at Marden, four miles north of the cathedral city. Here a three-sided polygonal apse was created, perhaps a design inspired by the lost Lady Chapel of Tewkesbury Abbey, of which the chancel seems to have been a simplified version (*see p. 38*). The reason for the grandiose rebuilding may have been Marden's significance as the first burial place of the murdered St Ethelbert, before the translation of his remains to Hereford itself. Elsewhere in the county, the chancels at Lyonshall and Dilwyn were both rebuilt, on more conventional lines, by Wormsley priory, again following appropriation, and in the latter case shortly before 1305, when in a dispute involving the vicar it was referred to as 'newly built'.[3] The chancel at Wigmore was likewise rebuilt in the early fourteenth century, presumably in this case by the neighbouring priory of Wigmore, which held the advowson.

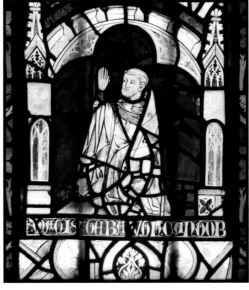

Eaton Bishop church: two details from the five-light east window, showing the Virgin and Child from the middle of the left-hand light (*left*) and Adam Murimuth from the bottom of central light (*right*)

At Eaton Bishop, a church of the bishops of Hereford, there seems to have been a two-stage rebuilding, the first carried out at the turn of the century, which saw the main work of construction, and the second some 20 or 30 years later, which took in the commissioning of a magnificent new east window.[4] The glass in the window, which survives complete, is superb and includes, in the middle row, figures of the Virgin and Child, St Michael, a bishop and St Gabriel and above, in the central light, a Crucifixion.[5] At the foot of the window is a row of donor figures, the central one of whom, dressed in a doctor's robes, is identified by name as Adam Murimuth, the chronicler, and a canon of Hereford and the bishop's proctor in Rome.[6] Murimuth's presence in the window presents some difficulty, as he is not actually recorded as an incumbent of the parish. The church which he held as a prebendary of Hereford was that of Bullinghope some five miles to the east.[7] It is possible that one of the rectors of the time, perhaps John de Orleton, Bishop Orleton's brother, organised a fundraising campaign, and that Murimuth contributed on condition that he was represented. Some years later, Bishop Grandison of Exeter was gently to chide Murimuth for his excessive ambition: an ambition which may have stretched to vanity.[8]

Chantries and side chapels

It was not so much in the construction or embellishment of chancels, however, that ecclesiastical patrons were to show themselves at their most active in Herefordshire. Surprisingly, perhaps, it was rather in the building of other parts of the church.

It may very well be the involvement of a cathedral or diocesan official, perhaps even the bishop, that accounts for the splendour of one of the most remarkable buildings of these years, the outer north chapel at Ledbury, an ambitious two-bay structure, lit by large four-light windows, all of them encrusted with decoration. Why this extraordinary chapel was built, and by whom, are both matters that have been much debated. The chapel is devoid of such liturgical fittings as a piscina, which could indicate the presence at one time of an altar, and there is no evidence that it was ever used for burials. It has been suggested that it was built to accommodate a relic of St Radegund, whose cult was later to be associated with the church, and the provision of separate visitor access in the south-west corner might well offer support for this view.[9] There are signs that an elite Hereford labour force was recruited to work on the project, as the windows are adorned by ballflower ornament, which recalls the similar feature on the cathedral tower. There was no shortage of links between Ledbury and the cathedral, as the manor was a property of the bishop and the two incumbents, or portionaries, of the church were both appointed by him. It has recently been suggested that

Ledbury church: east elevation of the outer north chapel

Dean Jean d'Aigueblanche could have been the patron, on the grounds that he left a bequest in his will for the roofing of a chapel in the church.[10] It is unlikely, however, that such could have been the case, as the bequest occurs too early: d'Aigueblanche's will was made in 1320, while the chapel could hardly have been begun before 1330.[11] Quite possibly it was the bishop himself who put up the money.

Senior or richly beneficed clergy were also responsible for some of the many perpetual chantry foundations made in these years. In 1307 John de Ross, a graduate of Oxford, canon of Hereford and a future bishop of Carlisle, founded a chantry in the church at Ross-on-Wye, his home town, for a chaplain to celebrate divine service in perpetuity.[12] The foundation was probably accommodated in a chapel in the south aisle, which was itself rebuilt at this time with rich ballflower decoration. A year before, Philip Talbot, archdeacon of Shropshire and another canon of Hereford, had founded a chantry in the church at Credenhill, to which he had been presented 20 years earlier by his kinsman Sir Richard Talbot, building a projecting chapel on the north side to accommodate it. Philip's responsibility for the project, according to Silas Taylor who visited the church in the 1650s, was attested by the words 'Phillipus Talbot me fecit' at the foot of one of the windows.[13] The chapel is unfortunately now lost. That Master Philip's piety was at least in some degree shaped by his response to the cult of St Thomas de Cantilupe is suggested by what we know of the glazing scheme which once graced the windows of the church. According to Taylor again, in the north chapel, which accommodated Philip's chantry, there was a window with the figure of the Virgin Mary and, in the light adjacent to it, that of an unidentified armed man with, above them, the arms of Talbot (gules a lion rampant, a border engrailed). At the top of the chancel east window were again the arms of Talbot, and in the second window on the chancel's south side, where they still remain, the figures of Thomas de Cantilupe and England's most celebrated canonised prelate, St Thomas Becket (*see p. 64*).[14] There can scarcely be any doubt that all three of these windows were commissioned by Talbot. Not only is there the evidence of the Talbot heraldry afforded us by Taylor; in style and technique the surviving panels of Cantilupe and Becket, which were clearly part of one and the same scheme, belong to the opening years of the fourteenth century, the years of Talbot's incumbency.[15] Since Cantilupe's canonisation was not actually to be approved until 1320, we are afforded a striking example of unofficial canonisation – that is, the elevation of a respected local figure to sainthood by popular acclaim. Quite possibly, Philip himself was active in promoting the cult locally, given his family's association with the see and his own possession of a stall in the cathedral.

Two other, less exalted Herefordshire clerks who founded perpetual chantries in this period were John Boter, vicar of Knightwick (Worcs) and a future treasurer of

Hereford Cathedral, who in 1332 established a foundation at King's Pyon (probably his birthplace), and Gregory atte Mulne, who a decade later was to do the same at Much Cowarne.[16] At King's Pyon a transeptal chapel was added to the south side of the church no later than the early fourteenth century, presumably to house a chantry, but it is not altogether clear whether this was for the foundation initiated by Boter. In the second half of the century the chapel was to be taken over as the burial place of the family of the lords of the manor. At Much Cowarne, a church under the influence of the Pauncefot family, there is no evidence that any alterations were made to the fabric of the church as a result of the foundation.

Ecclesiastical patronage of church building can be taken, in a broad sense, to include also the projects of well-to-do laymen closely related to senior churchmen and whose fortunes were intimately associated with theirs. In this category we may number as perhaps the most noteworthy patrons the Dunre (or Dinedor) family of Chilston in Madley, kinfolk of Bishop Swinfield by virtue of the marriage into the family of the bishop's niece, Margery. Swinfield, who was Cantilupe's secretary before he succeeded to the see, was probably a native of Kent, his name suggesting that his forebears were residents of the village of Swingfield near Folkestone. After his election he gathered his family around him, securing places in the chapter for his nephews John and Gilbert, who rose to be precentor and chancellor respectively, and establishing his father and elder brother, both called Stephen, as minor land-owners in the county.[17] The elder Stephen appears to have lived at Bosbury, where he may have held a preferential lease on the manor, dying there in the year that his son became bishop. His younger namesake established himself at Chilston by virtue of a feudal windfall, namely the bishop's grant to him of the wardship of a tenant of the see, Walter, son and heir of Sir Walter de Dunre of Chilston.[18] Stephen quickly secured the hand of the younger Walter for his daughter Margery and, his other children being celibate, it was Margery and her Dunre offspring who were to be bearers of Swinfield family memory. A generation later their son Richard and his wife, Agnes, were to establish a chantry in the cathedral for two chaplains to pray in perpetuity for their good estate so long as they were alive, their souls when they were dead, and for the soul of Richard Swinfield, sometime bishop of Hereford.[19]

St Mary's, Madley, mother church of the hamlet of Chilston and a possession of the chapter of Hereford, was the subject of an extensive rebuilding programme at this time which was to make it one of the largest and finest churches of the diocese. The church had already been remodelled in the early thirteenth century, shortly after its acquisition by the chapter, when the nave, aisles and tower were all rebuilt.[20] A century later a second major campaign was launched, apparently in response to the growth of a cult centring on a statue of the Virgin in the church, which made it a considerable centre of pilgrimage.[21] Under the leadership of a Hereford-trained mason the chancel was rebuilt on a larger scale with a magnificent apsidal east end while, beneath, a crypt was created to a similar plan, in which presumably the statue was displayed. These two programmes of works together appear to have been undertaken almost entirely by the dean and chapter, the second financed partly from offerings made at the statue.

Shortly after completion of the chancel, perhaps around 1330, work was commenced on an altogether new project, one unconnected with the others, the construction of the so-called Chilston chapel, in reality an outer aisle added to the south side of the nave (*see pp.* 22–23). This lavish structure, designed by the same mason as had worked on the chancel, is separated from the inner aisle by a fine five-bay arcade and is lit by a five-light east window and an even row of five three-light windows on the south side.[22] It is a commission notable as much for its size as for its opulence. Strangely, however, there is no evidence to indicate either why it was built or who could have paid for it. There are no documentary sources illuminating its construction, and the antiquarian record, otherwise so extensive for the church, sheds no light. The only clue is afforded by the name by which it is generally known, the Chilston chapel, attested from the seventeenth century, which points to a connection with the hamlet of

Madley church: view south across the nave to the Chilston aisle

Chilston in the parish, and so to the proprietorship of the Dunre family, who were its lords.[23] The Dunres, the one gentry family of any consequence in the parish, are the only people who can plausibly be credited with its construction. The most convincing explanation is that they built it to accommodate a second chantry foundation, a complement to the one which they had established in the cathedral. There is no indication that they had in mind making the chapel a family burial place. The Dunres were probably interred in the cathedral, in that north-eastern corner, close to Cantilupe's intended shrine, where Bishop Swinfield had started to create a family mausoleum. They appear to have been a family with a strong sense of ancestral memory.[24] They were by no means territorially well endowed, their inheritance stretching only to two manors, those of Chilston itself and Dinedor, to the south-east of Hereford. But they were almost certainly cash-rich.[25] The evidence of Madley suggests that in their role as architectural patrons they were able to punch well above their weight.

The difficulties we encounter in identifying responsibility for the Chilston aisle highlight a more general problem posed by discussion of architectural patronage in the Middle Ages: namely, the awkward lack of documentary evidence for its exercise. As we have seen, there are no extant contracts for any works undertaken in the county and diocese in the fourteenth century, nor are there fabric accounts for any building other than the cathedral. As a result, the identity of the patrons responsible for a project can only be inferred, although admittedly with a fair degree of probability in many cases. The most helpful pointer is usually afforded by ownership of the advowson, as it was with the advowson holder that responsibility ultimately lay for maintenance of the fabric. Where the building project consisted principally of the construction of a chantry chapel, however, it is possible that there may be a mortmain licence, authorising the transfer of lands to the foundation and recording the patron's name and the date of his initiative. For some of the grander projects of the period there may also, as at Credenhill, be the evidence of heraldry in the stained glass windows – or, if perhaps the glass itself has gone, then a record of it made by a local antiquary. In the case of a few more projects, there may be the evidence of the patrons' tomb effigies in recesses cut low into the walls. Between them, these sources are likely to shed light on who was responsible for a fair number of the projects undertaken in this period.

One important qualification needs to be made, however, and that is that they rarely if ever illuminate the contribution made by the local parishioners. Even where a project was initiated by someone of high rank – the lord of the manor or an institutional advowson holder – it may well have been finished off by the parish, perhaps as a result of a bargain struck at the beginning. Identifying the contribution made by the parishioners as a body is virtually impossible in an age, such as this, before the systematic compilation of churchwardens' accounts.

All these points need to be borne in mind when we turn from the patronage of building by the churchmen and their kin to works undertaken by the laity. In this latter category pride of place must be given to the activities of the Mortimer family, by far the most important resident landowning family not only in Herefordshire but in the whole of the central March.

5

The Unlikely Patrons: The Mortimers

The Mortimers' church building

A MONG THE LAITY involved in church building in and around Herefordshire in the fourteenth century, it is the Mortimers who must inevitably claim our attention first. The family were by far the richest and most important of the nobility of the central March, exercising wide social and political influence in the area. They also had the gift of appointment to a considerable number of local benefices. They had the potential to exercise a wide influence on the pace of church building in Herefordshire and south Shropshire.

By the beginning of the fourteenth century the family had been established at Wigmore for more than eight generations. Among the first of the Norman settlers in the March, they could trace their dominance back to an initial endowment made in the 1070s. Over the centuries they were able to add steadily to their holdings, in the twelfth century by seizing the Welsh cantrefs of Maelienydd and Elfael and later through acquisition of extensive lands in the Marches by marriage. The family's biggest early advances were made in the time of Sir Roger (d.1282), an assertive man, a royalist in the Baronial Wars, and an associate of Edward I, who was to establish himself as a major force in national politics. Through his brilliant marriage to the heiress Maud de Braose Sir Roger acquired a large Marcher endowment which included the lordships of Radnor and Narberth and a moiety of St Clears; and to these estates he was to add a grant of the lordships of Ceri and Cydewain from the Crown in 1279 and a further grant of Chirk to his younger son, Roger, in 1282.[1] A second good marriage was to assist the family's fortunes in the next but one generation, when a match between Sir Edmund Mortimer's son, another Roger, and Joan, heiress of the wealthy Geneville family, brought the Mortimers Ludlow Castle in Shropshire, additional lands in Herefordshire and the lordships of Trim and Meath in Ireland. Roger, an able but unscrupulous man who secured for himself the title earl of March, was to use the favour he enjoyed as the queen's paramour in the 1320s to build a dominant position nationally in both lands and offices. Although the family were to suffer a sharp reverse after Roger's overthrow and execution in 1330, the gains they had made were not permanently lost, and a recovery was to occur in the middle years of Edward III's reign.[2] Like their allies, the Berkeleys in Gloucestershire, the family were fertile in the production of sons, and they were able to establish a number of cadet lines, among these the branches seated at Chelmarsh (Salop) and Chirk (Denbighshire). Another Mortimer line, more distantly related but almost certainly still of shared ancestry, was seated at Richard's Castle. In the manner of the feudal nobility the Mortimers established an honorial monastery, in their case at Wigmore, close to the castle, in 1172, which was to serve as the family burial place. The family were also patrons of the small Herefordshire houses of Limebrook and Aconbury.

The Mortimers' extensive lordships in Herefordshire and thereabouts afforded them ample opportunities for religious patronage. Between them, the family's many branches disposed of over a dozen advowsons, among these the right to appoint to the churches of Pembridge, Kingsland, Tedstone Wafer, Thornbury and Winforton (all Heref.), Hopton Wafers and Neen Sollars (Salop) and Radnor (Wales). Other advowsons again, such as those of Leintwardine and Presteigne, were in the gift of the family foundation of Wigmore Abbey.

Pembridge church and its detached tower from the south-east

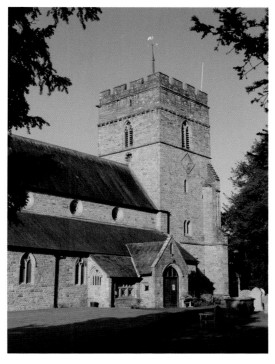

Kingsland church from the south-east

The two most impressive instances of the family's patronage of building are afforded by the two end-to-end rebuildings of the churches of Pembridge and Kingsland, both in the family heartland in the north-west of the county. The rebuilding of Pembridge, undertaken on an especially expansive scale, may have been occasioned by the family's desire to enhance the dignity and standing of the small town, which a predecessor of theirs, in 1239, had raised to borough status.[3] Members of the family resided intermittently in a motte-and-bailey castle just to the south of the church, and Roger, the future first earl, and his wife, were married there in 1301.[4] At Kingsland the rebuilding, begun a few years after Pembridge, was again quite ambitious, and apparently the work of a mason of Bristol origin who delighted in the use of such Bristol motifs as triangles and polygonal door-heads (*see p. 42*).

The Mortimers were almost certainly responsible for a third near-total rebuilding, at Orleton, another of their properties, where a nave of the second quarter of the century survives, although the chancel has been replaced.[5] An interesting feature of the design is the inclusion of a series of carved heads, including those of a king and a queen and two mitred churchmen. The figures of the king and queen may be representations of the young Edward III, who had come to the throne in 1327, and his wife Philippa of Hainault. The family appears to have undertaken a fourth rebuilding at Neen Sollars, just over the county boundary into Shropshire. In 1287 they had acquired the advowson of this church, and they oversaw the rebuilding of its fabric some 20 or 30 years later.[6] Although the plan of the church breathes some ambition

Orleton church: head of a queen, possibly Philippa of Hainault, wife of Edward III

with its cruciform shape and central tower, the work is poorly executed, and the cost of the project may have been shared with the parish. Just over the county boundary into Wales there was a substantial rebuilding of the main vessel of the nave at Presteigne, another important Mortimer property and the site of a castle.

Leintwardine church: the large chantry chapel on the north side of the chancel (*left*)

On a lesser scale were two commissions for which Roger, the first earl, was responsible in his years of pomp. Both were chantry foundations and both were inaugurated in 1328, two years before his downfall, the first in Leintwardine church and the second in Ludlow Castle.[7] At Leintwardine Mortimer's foundation was an ambitious one, with no fewer than nine chaplains provided for to pray in perpetuity for the souls of the king and queen, Henry, bishop of Lincoln and the Mortimers themselves and their ancestors and successors. To accommodate the foundation, Mortimer constructed a chapel adjacent to the chancel with three two-light windows on the north side and a big four-light window on the east.[8] In Ludlow Castle Mortimer provided for his priestly community by building an entirely new chapel in the outer bailey, of which one window with characteristic Herefordshire Y-tracery survives. Mortimer also appears to have been responsible for the construction of a chapel of a similar date on the north side of the church at Cleobury Mortimer (Salop), yet another family property.[9] This is of two bays and is also likely to have housed a chantry foundation.

Top left: Ludlow Castle (Salop): blocked window with Y-tracery, in the former chantry chapel
Top right: Richard's Castle church: three-light east window in the south aisle, with ballflower decoration
Above: Richard's Castle church: capital belonging to the south aisle, again with ballflower

A couple of substantial church building projects can be associated with junior branches of the Mortimer family. At Richard's Castle, a church high up in the bailey of the castle from which the village takes its name, a south aisle was added to the nave in the 1310s, probably at the behest of Joan, daughter and co-heiress of Hugh de Mortimer, the last male representative of his line (*see p. 38*). In a second phase of building, undertaken some 40 years later, the chancel was rebuilt and a north transept added, to accommodate a chantry. These later works were probably initiated by Sir John Talbot, Joan's son by her second marriage.[10] To the north-east, in Shropshire, an end-to-end rebuilding was undertaken by another cadet of the family, Sir Hugh Mortimer of Chelmarsh, who in the 1340s rebuilt Chelmarsh church to accommodate a chantry foundation, commissioning a simple but effective design with nave and chancel under a single roof (*see p. 30*). The master mason employed here was a local man who also worked on the neighbouring churches of Kinlet and Stottesdon.[11]

Of all these projects, the rebuilding of Pembridge church stands out as perhaps the most impressive. The church, big, wide and bulky, presents a splendid sight on approach from the former market place, standing high in its elevated churchyard. To its left is the detached bell tower, the timberwork of which dates from the thirteenth century. The Mortimers' new fabric was begun no later than 1330, and to judge from its stylistic unity must have been completed fairly quickly. The evidence of the masons'

Pembridge church and its detached tower from the south-west

marks still visible on the fabric points to a building period of no more than about four years for the nave and transepts, with some eight or nine skilled masons working at any one time.[12] It seems likely that the whole church, excepting the porch which came later, would have been finished in under a decade. The building was conceived to an ambitious plan, consisting of a tall nave with aisles and widely spaced bays, lower north and south transepts and low chancel (*see p. 19*). Designed by a mason who was almost certainly locally based, but nonetheless aware of the latest architectural currents at Tewkesbury, it constitutes a fluent essay in the Decorated style and is adorned with the distinctive feature of porthole windows in the clerestory. The arms of the Mortimers, and of the Geneville and Grandison families to whom they were related, once featured in the windows, attesting to close family interest in the church.[13]

After Pembridge, perhaps the finest of the Mortimers' churches is that found at Kingsland, another sizeable building and not unlike Pembridge internally, although without the latter's projecting transepts. As we have seen, the church is the work of a mason apparently trained at Bristol, who delighted in the use of such Bristol motifs as triangles and polygonal door-heads (*see p. 42*). A peculiarity of the building is the presence alongside the north porch of a small chapel, the so-called Volka chapel, which has on its south side a tomb recess and was probably the burial place of a junior member of the Mortimer family.[14] The chapel is notable for its curious north window made up of two stages, the upper one of six straight-sided lights and the lower of three square panels with octofoils. As at Pembridge, Mortimer heraldry was once a notable feature of the stained glass windows.[15]

Kingsland church: canopied tomb recess in the south wall of the Volka Chapel

A female strain of piety?

This extensive range of commissions suggests that there may be a case for reassessing conventional interpretations of the Mortimer family's piety. The Mortimers are a line not hitherto singled out for the range and generosity of their religious patronage.

Kingsland church: the Volka Chapel

According to Charles Hopkinson, 'there is scant evidence of any religious benefactions' by the most famous member of the family Roger, the first earl, with the exception of the chapel in the bailey of Ludlow Castle, which the Wigmore chronicle says that he founded. While conceding that Roger was responsible for a substantial chantry foundation at Leintwardine, Hopkinson nonetheless adds that 'he felt little need to court' the favour of ecclesiastics, being assured of the crucial support of Adam Orleton, bishop of Hereford.[16] It has also been observed that the Mortimers undertook little or no work at Wigmore Abbey, the family's honorial foundation, in this period.[17]

To dismiss the family's religious patronage in such terms, however, may be to do both them and their kin an injustice. It would certainly be to take insufficient account of the considerable interest that the family took in the parish churches in their gift. In this sphere, the evidence of their patronage is abundant.

Various members of the Mortimer line seem to have been responsible for initiating the building programmes we have been considering. Perhaps the unlikeliest was the first earl himself, Roger IV, a man rightly identified as motivated largely by material considerations. His patronage, however, took an entirely predictable form: it manifested itself in chantry foundations – that is, in the establishment of intercessory institutions designed to safeguard his good estate while he lived, and the safety of his and his family's souls after their deaths. To found a chantry was to take out a sort of spiritual insurance policy. It might perhaps be said that if anyone in the fourteenth century was in need of such a policy, it was Earl Roger.

The others in the direct line of the family, who stand out as being active in their patronage of church building are the well-to-do womenfolk. It is highly tempting to associate the work at no fewer than four of the churches – those of Pembridge, Kingsland, Orleton and Presteigne – with Margaret (née Fiennes), the long-lived widow of Earl Roger's father, Sir Edmund. After the death of her husband in 1304, Margaret was to hold all four of the properties as part of the extensive jointure which she had in the Mortimer estates, effectively barring her son from access to a large part of the family's wealth. Margaret was to survive until 1334.[18] In the case of Pembridge and Kingsland, the two biggest undertakings, we should perhaps also allow for the involvement of Margaret's successor in the two properties, Joan de Geneville (d.1356), widow of the first earl.[19] It was almost certainly Joan who saw the projects through to completion. The four properties were thus ones which, in the key period, were controlled by women. At Kingsland the presence of the Bristol-derived features in the building can be explained by the involvement of yet another of the womenfolk, Margaret (d.1337), eldest daughter of Earl Roger, who was given in marriage to Thomas III, Lord Berkeley, a wealthy Gloucestershire landowner and an ally of the Mortimers. The Berkeleys were hereditary patrons of

St Augustine's Abbey, Bristol (now Bristol Cathedral), and all the Bristol-derived features at Kingsland are ones which had earlier featured at St Augustine's.[20] It might be possible to detect still further female interest in parochial patronage in the burial choice made by another lady of the family again, Blanche, youngest daughter of Roger, the first earl, who was married to the Herefordshire banneret, Peter, Lord Grandison. On her death in 1347 Blanche was laid to rest in the parish church of Much Marcle, another of the Mortimer family's manors (see p. 51). At Richard's Castle it is likely that the patron responsible for the first phase of building, the construction of a new south aisle, was Joan (d.1340), daughter and coheiress of Hugh, the last of his line. It is hardly coincidental that female influence in the affairs of the main, Wigmore, branch of the family should have been so pronounced from 1332, when, after the death of Roger's son and heir, Edmund, there was a long minority before the coming of age of Roger, the second earl. In these years it was the two long-lived dowagers who seized control of the family's cultural and religious patronage and directed it to the parish churches in their gift.

The involvement of wealthy aristocratic women and, most of all, of amply-dowered widows is a widely recognised feature of the religious patronage of the late Middle Ages. It has been noted in the case of many other noble and gentry families of the period. At North Leigh (Oxon), for example, in the 1430s Elizabeth, widow of the lawyer William Wilcotes, was to honour the memory of her deceased husband by raising a magnificent tomb to his memory and building next to it a beautiful, fan-vaulted chapel in which Masses were to be said for his soul. At Tong (Salop), 20 years earlier, Isabella, widow of Sir Fulk de Pembridge, went much further, completely rebuilding the church and endowing a whole community of chaplains to pray for the souls of her three deceased husbands. Tong church is one of the finest examples of Perpendicular architecture in the West Midlands (see p. 112). At Lingfield (Surrey) in the 1360s, after the death of her husband, Sir Reginald, Joan, Lady Cobham, undertook the building of a new Lady Chapel on the north side of the church, while 70 years later a successor of hers, Anne, the widow of a later Cobham, ended up rebuilding the rest of the fabric to match it.

Many other examples can be cited of aristocratic ladies engaging in church building in the late medieval period. Mention might be made of the involvement of Alice, duchess of Suffolk (d.1475), in the rebuilding of Ewelme church (Oxon) and the endowment of the almshouse next to it. One big difference, however, is to be noticed between the patronage of these ladies and that of the ladies of the Mortimer family. The generosity shown by these other aristocratic women was occasioned in each case by the establishment of a major intercessory foundation. Even at Lingfield, Anne, Lady Cobham, when she rebuilt the church, was founding a chantry college to go with it. There is no sign at all that the founding and endowment of a chantry or college was what prompted the generosity of Margaret or any other of the Mortimer ladies. In none of the churches, either wholly or partly rebuilt by them in these years, is there any record of a chantry being established. Nor is there any evidence, as there is in the other examples cited, of the act of rebuilding being associated with making grander provision for burial. All but one of the representatives of the main line of the Mortimer family were buried, so far as we know, at Wigmore Abbey, the family mausoleum. Although there is a high status monument in the Volka Chapel at Kingsland, which may perhaps commemorate Walter Mortimer, rector between 1304 and about 1328 (see p. 81), there is no indication that his burial was connected with the rebuilding of the church.[21] Commissioning of the tomb appears to have been the result of a quite separate initiative.

A possible clue to what lay behind the Mortimer ladies' endeavours is afforded by the choice of churches on which they spent the most lavish sums, those of Pembridge and Kingsland. Both churches lay immediately adjacent to a Mortimer residence. At Pembridge the old motte-and-bailey castle adjoined the churchyard to the south, on the site now occupied by Court House Farm, while at Kingsland it lay a little to the west. At both sites remains of earthworks are still to be seen. In a sense, the two churches can be seen as acting in the office of castle chapels. They were extensions of the apparatus of Mortimer power and lordship. At Pembridge the newly rebuilt church set the seal on the semi-urban status of the aspirant manorial borough at its feet. Unsurprisingly, ample provision was made in the rebuilt fabrics for the display of Mortimer heraldry in the stained glass windows. In the 1640s Richard Symonds was to record that in the chancel windows at Pembridge there were the arms not only of the Mortimers but also of the Genevilles, into whom they had married, and in the north transept those of the Grandisons, to whom they were also related.[22] At Kingsland there were the arms of the Mortimers again, and those of the de Braoses, another family into whom they had married.[23] At Pembridge, another feature pointing to close Mortimer interest is the remarkable gallery of carved heads, not dissimilar to that at Orleton. One of the heads may be a representation of Roger Mortimer while two others appear to be likenesses of Edward III and his queen, Philippa of Hainault.[24] The churches of Pembridge and Kingsland, therefore, can hardly be considered ordinary parish churches. They were buildings which were turned by their patrons into theatres of display, sites in which the apparatus of visual display could be deployed to promote Mortimer lordship and power.

Considerations of this sort certainly go a long way to explaining the close interest which the Mortimer ladies and, in particular, the first Margaret took in the two churches by their castle gates. They do not, however, do a great deal to explain the interest which they and other members of the family took in the other churches on which attention was lavished. While a desire to promote family power accounts for the scale of the two grandest churches they commissioned, we must also allow that various broader considerations were involved in the patronage of church building.

In a general sense, the family's interest in the parish churches on their manors can be seen as one aspect of the growing awareness on the part of the late medieval nobility and gentry of a parochial dimension to the exercise of lordship. Lordship, it was believed, was a divinely ordained institution, part of the eternal hierarchy of authority, in which rule over the manor might merge imperceptibly into rule over the parish. Family influence would naturally be felt most strongly in those parishes where, as at Pembridge, Kingsland and Neen Sollars, the lord of the manor was also the holder of the advowson. In his capacity as patron, the lord would be responsible not only for nominating the incumbent but also for championing the parishioners' interests in disputes with outside authorities and for assisting them with the cost of building repairs and the provision of fixtures and fittings. In synodal legislation in the thirteenth century the laity had been assigned responsibility for maintaining the fabric of much of the church and for providing a wide range of liturgical equipment. Where, as in poorer and more thinly populated parishes, the parishioners were lacking in means, it would be the lord or lady who would have to step in to make good the deficit. The evidence of aristocratic testamentary bequests suggests that on the whole these people were not unwilling to share in that responsibility. While the lack of evidence of this sort for the Mortimers makes it difficult to track their own generosity in bequests, the physical evidence of their patronage of church building is telling. That it should have been principally the womenfolk who were active as builders is a consequence simply of the fact that they were most often in residence on their estates. Unlike their menfolk, they did not travel a great deal: they were not involved in affairs of state; nor were they affected by the demands of war. They had both the opportunity and, in the case of widows, the means to indulge their patronage. Among the ladies of the Mortimer family, it is Margaret, Sir Edmund's long-lived widow, who emerges as the outstanding patron.

6

The Gentry and the Townsmen

I F THE MORTIMERS were much the grandest family in Herefordshire in the fourteenth century, the greater part of the county's landed wealth lay in the hands of the gentry: the knights and esquires, those just below the nobility in rank. Numbering some two dozen resident families, they comprised a fairly self-contained group who held few of their lands outside the county and who regularly intermarried and looked to one another for mutual support.

The pattern of gentry church building

In terms of the number of projects they undertook, it was the gentry who left by far the biggest mark on the county's churches in this period. The bishop and the dean and chapter of Hereford and the county's monastic proprietors, although owning a considerable number of churches between them, were not especially active as builders. Unlike, for example, their counterparts in Shropshire, the monks of Shrewsbury, they do not appear to have been enthusiastic about paying for the construction of ambitious new chancels.[1] The local gentry, by contrast, left their imprint in one way or another on a large number of the county's fabrics. Admittedly, they undertook few end-to-end rebuildings; and those which they did undertake were fairly modest in scale. At Ashperton, their chief seat, and at Stretton Grandison nearby, the Grandisons, who hovered on the edge of the nobility, were responsible for two medium-scale reconstructions, the latter church being the bigger of the two, and dignified externally with a tall west tower and spire. At Almeley the Pychards were responsible for rebuilding the greater part of the church, the chancel in the 1290s and the nave perhaps 20 years later (*see overleaf*). At Croft a member of the de Croft family, perhaps their most active member, Sir Hugh (d.1317), substantially rebuilt the church there, a modest building close to the family manor house.[2] At Kinnersley, another church next to a manor house, a stage-by-stage reconstruction begun early in the century by the de Kinnersleys

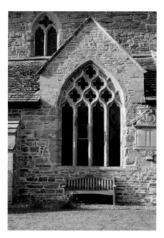

Top left: Almeley church: reticulated tracery in the window of the south aisle gabled bay.
Top right: Almeley church from the south-east. *Above*: Amberley chapel near Marden

and finished off by their de la Bere successors led to the near-total replacement of the earlier fabric. At Amberley, near Marden, the modest free-standing chapel adjacent to the manor house was completely rebuilt by the family who owned it, probably a branch of the de Lingens. Still in use, the chapel constitutes a rare surviving example of this type of building. Outside the county, at Crickhowell, the Pauncefots, a substantial landowning line in both Herefordshire and mid-Wales, were responsible for constructing an entirely new cruciform church to dignify the town of their Marcher lordship.[3] Last, but not least, in Shropshire in the 1340s Sir Hugh Mortimer, head of a Mortimer cadet line, was responsible for the complete rebuilding of Chelmarsh church, albeit on a more modest scale.

At other churches the work undertaken was generally less ambitious and far-reaching, in many cases taking the form of additions or extensions to accommodate chantry foundations. At Stretford, another church in the gift of the de la Beres, a short eastward extension of both chancel and aisle was carried out, probably to accommodate family burials. At Richard's Castle, as we have seen, first a south aisle was added and then, shortly after the Black Death, a north transept constructed near the junction of nave and chancel. Transept chapels were also added to the churches at Clehonger, Dilwyn, Yazor, Fownhope, King's Pyon and Credenhill. At Bishopstone and Ashperton a transept was eventually thrown out on each side, so as to produce a cruciform plan. At Sarnesfield the addition took the form not of a projecting chapel but of a short flanking aisle to the south of the chancel. At Much Cowarne an existing aisle on the south side of the nave was taken down and rebuilt.[4] In at least one case, where extra space was needed, the patron, instead of building a new chapel, simply appropriated an existing one, presumably by this time defunct, adapting it to his own use. This appears to have been what happened at Dilwyn where a chapel, originally built by either the Tyrells or the Audleys, was taken over by the de la Beres.[5]

At Little Hereford, on the banks of the Teme, it was the chancel that was rebuilt and enlarged to accommodate high-status family burials. The provision made here by the local lords, the de la Mare family, whose moated manor house stood close by, was lavish. Against the north wall two impressive conjoined tomb recesses were

Little Hereford church: the small, doorway-like chancel arch (*left*).
Pair of tomb recesses on the north side of the chancel (*right*)

King's Pyon church: the early fourteenth-century nave roof

constructed, each with a cusped arch and a crocketed ogee gable, and each supported on semi-octagonal panelled pedestals. In the eastern recess was laid the finely
carved incised slab of a de la Mare lady, which is still extant. The chancel's character
as principally a family burial space, the preserve of the lord of the manor and his
close relations, is reinforced by the tiny arch which separates it from the nave.

In virtually all the cases discussed, the builder concerned was both lord of the
manor and holder of the advowson. Sometimes, however, a collaboration can be
sensed between the lord and another party, be that either the parish community or
the advowson holder if someone other than the lord. At Pembridge the Gours of
Marston, tenants and servants of the Mortimer family, may have borne some of the
cost of building the north transept of the new church, if the presence there at one
time of their tombs, dating from the later fourteenth century, can be taken as indicative of their interest (*see p. 53*).[6] At King's Pyon, the signs are that the remodelling
of the nave formed part of a bargain which the lord, Sir Gerard de Eylesford, struck
with neighbouring Wormsley priory when he made over the advowson to the house
in 1311.[7] It is hardly coincidental that the nave and south chapel of the church with
their spectacular timber roofs should date from around the time of the transfer,
the opening decades of the fourteenth century.[8] Quite possibly, the arrangement
was that the priory would meet part of the cost of the project as a condition of Sir
Gerard granting them the living, which was a reasonably valuable one.[9] A development later in the century at King's Pyon was the insertion of new fenestration into
the south chapel, and the adoption of that part of the church by the lord's family as
their preferred burial place. One of the tomb effigies now in a recess in the south
wall is to a member of the Mortimer family who held the manor in the 1380s.[10]

What sort of people were these knightly or gentry patrons, and what was their
standing in society? At the very top they overlapped with the ranks of the lesser
nobility. The wealthy de Grandisons, whose works we have already noted, actually
received summonses to parliament as lords, and probably enjoyed an income in the
order of £200 a year. Another county family, the de Verdons, were of similar rank
but became extinct in the second decade of the century after Sir Theobald, the last
of his line, died without issue, leaving his estates to be divided between his four
daughters and co-heiresses.[11] It was either the de Verdons or their successors who
were responsible for rebuilding the nave at Weobley, one of the family's main properties, and for constructing the north aisle at Ludlow, where the family's arms once
figured in the stained glass and where a surviving tomb recess may commemorate
a family member (*see pp. 38 and 40*).[12] At least one family which failed to maintain
its position in the baronage is represented – the Devereux, who, as a line of mere
knightly rank, were responsible for additions to Bodenham church. The Devereux

lost their position in the peerage after falling into debt and then being ensnared by the financial wiles of Edward I's notoriously corrupt Treasurer, Walter Langton, bishop of Coventry and Lichfield.[13] A lady of the family is commemorated in the chancel at Bodenham by a fine tomb monument on which she is shown with a young child at her side sheltered in the folds of her robe (*see p. 48*).

Many of the other church builders were busy, well-connected knights, men with incomes in the £40–£100 per annum bracket. At Fownhope the patron was Sir Roger Chandos, lord of the manor, scion of an old Herefordshire family, and owner of two other manors in the county in his own right and a string of manors in the south-west by right of his wife.[14] At Chelmarsh (Salop), as we have seen, the rebuilding was undertaken by Sir Hugh Mortimer, a cadet of the main line of the family and a proprietor with lands in three counties (*see p. 30*).[15] At Crickhowell and Stretford the rebuildings were again undertaken by substantial well-to-do families, the Pauncefots in the former case and the de la Beres in the latter (*see p. 49*).[16] At Kinnersley the later parts of the rebuilding were likewise undertaken by the de la Beres, seemingly an ambitious line.[17] For all the dominance of the wealthy, however, it is worth noting that a number of less well-to-do families are also represented. The de Kinnersleys, who rebuilt the earlier parts at Kinnersley, and the de Sarnesfields at Sarnesfield were both families whose landholdings appear to have been confined to a single manor.[18] The de Sarnesfields, however, for all the constraints of their income, were able both to afford a fine roof for their church and to commission some excellent stained glass to fill the windows.

Sarnesfield church: the south elevation (*left*) and interior looking east (*right*)

Most of Herefordshire's church-building proprietors were men (or women) who were both leaders of their communities and socially well connected. Some, such as the de la Mares of Little Hereford and the Daniels of Bishopstone, were tenants of the see of Hereford and performed military service on the bishop's behalf.[19] It is possible that the weeper knights shown on the sides of St Thomas de Cantilupe's shrine in Hereford Cathedral are to be interpreted as the see's knightly tenants, caught in the act of both honouring and mourning the bishop-saint. According to ancient custom, military service was due from the see for fourteen knights' fees – the service from another two-and-a-half being disputed; and fourteen is precisely the number of knights shown on the shrine (see p. 62).[20]

Other proprietors were magnate retainers. Sir Roger Tyrel, probably a builder at Dilwyn, was retained by the last de Clare earls of Gloucester, while Sir Roger Chandos, founder of a chantry at Fownhope and a hardy survivor in an unstable age, was a dependant of the earl of Hereford.[21] Other knights again, notably those from families in the west and north-west of the county, had either tenurial or retaining ties with the Mortimers of Wigmore.

Tomb effigy at Dilwyn church, probably of Sir Roger Tyrel

Quite a number of the group held office in county administration. Sir John le Rous, Sir Miles Pychard and Sir Roger Chandos all served at one time or another as sheriff, while Sir Grimbald Pauncefot, Sir Hugh de Croft, Sir John de la Mare, Hugh de Kinnersley, and Pychard and Chandos again were elected to parliament.[22] Especially close bonds are to be observed between two office-holders, Sir Richard de Pembridge and Sir Philip Clanvow, who were both appointed supervisors of the wool subsidy in 1340, and keepers of the peace from 1344.[23] Pembridge was to build a chantry chapel at Clehonger in 1342, and Clanvow one at Yazor five years later (see p. 53).[24] The bonds between this tightly-knit group of knights might originate in or be reinforced by the experience of shared military service. Sir Roger Tyrel and Sir John de la Mare had both fought in the Falkirk campaign of 1298, while Tyrel again, Sir John le Rous, Sir Gerard de Eylesford, Sir Roger Chandos, Sir Miles Pychard and Sir Hugh de Croft were all to see service in Scotland between 1305 and 1307; Croft, a man with a toehold in Shropshire, was to serve with Fulk, son of Sir Fulk Fitzwaryn, who is probably to be identified with the man of that name who built the fine chantry chapel at Alberbury in that county.[25] Later in the century, Sir Reginald de la Mare and Thomas de Sarnesfield were to enlist for the Crécy and Calais campaign of 1346.[26]

Most striking of all are the ties of neighbourhood which bound together so many of these men. Well over half of the proprietors who were active in church building held lands in the north of the county. Sir Roger Tyrel at Dilwyn, Sir Philip Clanvow at Yazor, the de Crofts at Croft, the de la Beres at Stretford, the de Kinnersleys at Kinnersley, the de la Mares at Little Hereford, and the Mortimers at Richard's Castle were all resident in the district broadly to the north and north-west of Leominster. South of this line lived the Devereux at Bodenham, the Pauncefots at Crickhowell and Much Cowarne, the Pychards at Letton and Almeley, the Pembridges at Clehonger and the Chandoses at Fownhope and Snodhill. Members of both groups of families were prominent in local society and had a range of ties with families in other parts of the county.[27] Most of the families who were most active in church building were members of a landowning community who were bound together by ties of association and proximity and whose members were of like interest, outlook and taste.

Tying the members of the group still more closely together were the bonds that many of them had with the Mortimer family, who were themselves rooted in the north-west of the county. The Pychards, de Kinnersleys, de la Mares, Pauncefots and Sarnesfields were all, in one or another of their manorial estates, tenants of the Mortimers.[28] At least one family married into the Mortimers, Sir Peter, the last of the de Grandison line, marrying Blanche, daughter of Roger, the first earl, and raising a fine monument to her memory at Much Marcle.[29] Many other members of the gentry had ties of association with the family. Sir Miles Pychard, Sir Hugh de Croft, Sir Walter Devereux, Sir Aymer Pauncefot and Hugh de Kinnersley, all of them friends or retainers of the family as well as neighbours, were at one time or another witnesses of their charters.[30] In 1320 no fewer than four of the group – Sir Roger Chandos, Sir Gerard de Eylesford, Sir Richard de Pembridge and John de Sarnesfield – acted as guarantors of the marriage of Roger Mortimer's daughter, Margaret, to Thomas de Berkeley III of Berkeley, while another, Sir Hugh de Croft, was a witness.[31] Ten years earlier two of the group, Croft and Kinnersley, had accompanied Mortimer on the expedition to Ireland in which he sought to re-establish his rights in the lands that had come to him by his marriage to the Geneville heiress; in 1317 Croft was actually to lose his life in Mortimer's service there.[32] For some at least of the group, in 1321 the shared experience of service to the Mortimers extended so far as to taking part with them in the rising against the king's favourites, the Despensers. In the autumn of that year Sir Thomas de la Bere, Sir Aymer Pauncefot, Sir Richard de Pembridge and John de Sarnesfield were all to receive pardons from the king at Mortimer's request for their role in the rising.[33] In 1322 Sarnesfield and Pauncefot and two of their neighbours – Reginald de la Mare and Philip Clanvow – were to suffer forfeiture of their lands for their part in the rebellion against the king.[34] So prominently does church building figure in the cultural activities of the group in the Mortimers' circle that among those close to the family only the Lingens do not appear in the church builders' ranks.[35] Whether or not the knights' own church building activities were influenced at all by those of the Mortimers is hard to determine. What can be said, however, is that for both the Mortimers and those who were associated with them church building constituted a shared form of cultural expression.

The townsmen

One final group who were heavily involved in church building in this period call for our attention, and that is the townsmen. The wealthy burgesses of the region's towns were just as active as the nobility and well beneficed clergy in adding to church fabrics and comprehensively improving them. At Hereford, the church of All Saints was almost completely rebuilt in the late thirteenth and early fourteenth centuries, in parts probably to the designs of a mason who also worked at Clehonger and Eaton Bishop. At the north-west corner of the building a tall, eye-catching tower was raised, crowned by an elegant ribbed spire set behind battlements and with big lucarnes at the foot. Substantial work was also undertaken at Hereford's other main church, St Peter's, an ancient collegiate foundation dating back to the late eleventh century. Here too a tower crowned by a tall spire was raised, in this case at the junction of the south aisle and south chapel, and around it the greater part of the fabric was rebuilt.[36] Outside Hereford, the most substantial building work was carried out at Leominster and Ledbury. At Leominster a new outer south aisle was added to the monastic church for the exclusive use of the parish, a work of considerable splendour with its west window and row of five south windows all studded with ballflower.

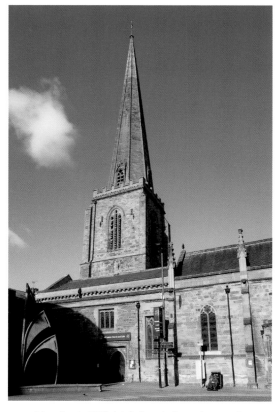

Hereford, All Saints' church from the south

At Ledbury the rebuilding of the north aisle, begun half-a-century earlier, was completed and the entire south aisle and chapel rebuilt to a unified design with elegant three-light windows. At Ross-on-Wye, too, substantial work was carried out on the aisles in the late thirteenth and early fourteenth centuries.[37]

Unfortunately, we are entirely lacking the sorts of documentary sources so essential if we are to identify the patrons of any of these works. For the period before the fifteenth century there are no surviving archives for any of Herefordshire's urban communities; nor are there any wills or churchwardens' accounts. At Ledbury and Leominster urban autonomy was anyway lacking, authority being exercised in the former town by the bishop and in the latter by the priory. In general, it is probably fair to say that most of the building work was carried out by members of the local mercantile elite acting either in a personal capacity or collectively through guilds. At all three churches outside Hereford the concentration of work on the side aisles points strongly to guild involvement, as aisles were often partitioned up for guild use.

While the townsmen or burgesses, however, are likely to have been responsible for the bulk of the work carried out in urban churches in this period, allowance should also be made for the possible involvement of other parties. We have already noted that at Ross-on-Wye a clerk, John de Ross, the future bishop of Carlisle, was the founder of a chantry and so very likely a part-contributor to the cost of the south aisle there.[38] We have also seen that the de Verdons, who were lesser nobility, were responsible for the north aisle of the nave at Ludlow (see p. 38). At Ledbury too there is good reason to suspect the involvement of a family which was not of burgess background. This was one of the most important gentry families of the county, the Pauncefots of Crickhowell and Much Cowarne, who had lands in the area. Their mark was left in the form of funerary sculpture.

Against the wall of the north chancel aisle at Ledbury, near the east end, is the fine tomb monument of a lady, not dissimilar in style to that at Much Marcle, and on the evidence of its heraldry clearly commemorating a Pauncefot lady. The tomb consists of the effigy of the lady herself, shown naturalistically with the train of her dress hanging over the edge, on top of a richly panelled chest with supports on each side, and with the first stage of an elaborate canopy rising behind (see p. 51). The superstructure of the canopy, which probably took the form of an open arcade in front of the window, is now lost. The arms on the shields running along the back panel are those of Pauncefot and Carew, suggesting that the lady commemorated may be Maud, sister of Sir Grimbald Pauncefot, and wife of Sir Thomas Carew (d.1334). The Pauncefots, who were extensive landowners in the Marches, also held the manor of Hazle on the edge of Ledbury, and they were later to be associated with a small chantry in the church.[39] This latter had originally been set up in the

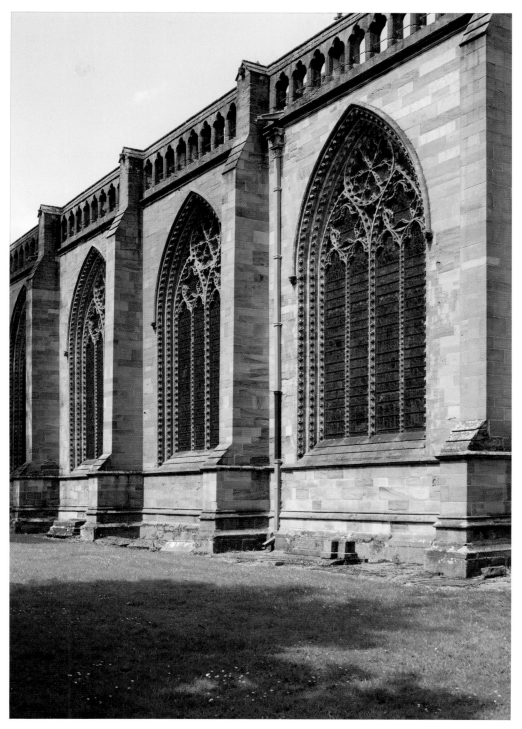

Leominster Priory: the south elevation

1350s by John le Hop of Ledbury and his wife, and it was to be re-established a generation later by the couple's executors, who were to include one Alice Pauncefot.[40] The suggestion has been made that the monument is not in its original position, and that it was originally placed on the opposite side of the church, where the later chantry was to be situated.[41] There is no evidence, however, to support this idea, and the design of the monument, which provides for an open-work superstructure, is ideally suited to its present position in front of a window.

Taken together, the evidence of Pauncefot interest in Ledbury church and the survival there of the Pauncefot monument afford a useful reminder of the considerable overlap between the two categories of gentry and townsfolk in the Middle Ages. The wealthier and more successful of the townsmen aspired to the distinction of blue-

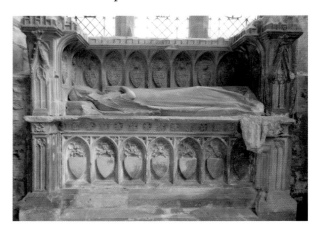

Ledbury church: the Pauncefot tomb

blooded gentility, while members of the rural gentry married into or were associated with the townsfolk. The two groups were not mutually exclusive; rather, their worlds intersected and overlapped. And so too it was with the ranks of the clerical estate and the burgesses; their worlds likewise overlapped and informed one another. When John de Ross, the future bishop of Carlisle, a lawyer and a royal diplomat, founded a chantry at Ross-on-Wye, he was implicitly acknowledging his origins in the well-to-do mercantile society of that town. It is worth remembering that the best known of all Herefordshire clerks of the period, Adam Orleton, the bishop of Hereford, despite his well-known associations with the noble family of Mortimer, was almost certainly born into a burgess family of Hereford.[42]

7

Paying the Bills

T HE FINANCIAL TERMS for any church building project would typically be set out in the indenture or contract entered into by both client and mason, in which details would be recorded of the nature of the project and arrangements made for payment.

As we have seen, no building contracts of this kind have come down to us from Herefordshire and the Central March for the period in which the Decorated style flourished. A rough idea of the probable scale of costs, however, can be gained from contracts that have survived from other parts of the country. From the eve of the Black Death, in 1348, we have a contract entered into by the dean and chapter of St Paul's Cathedral for the rebuilding of the chancel of Sandon church (Herts), for which the very reasonable sum of 20 marks (between £13 and £14) was agreed, along with the right allowed to the builder of taking away the materials of the old structure. From the early fifteenth century we have two contracts from Yorkshire. The first is an agreement made in January 1410 between John Conyers and Richard the mason of Newton for the building of an aisle and a three-bay arcade at Hornby church, for the sum of 51 marks, or about £34 – rather less than the minimum annual income required for knighthood. From two years later we have the agreement between the Burgh family, neighbours of Conyers, and the same mason for the end-to-end rebuilding of Catterick church at a cost of a little over £100.[1] These two early fifteenth-century contracts were entered into at a time when labour costs were rising. Fifty or sixty years earlier, before the Black Death, the cost of labour would have been cheaper. Building styles at the earlier time, however, were generally more elaborate. If these two variables can be said to cancel each other out, it is likely that overall costs in the two periods would probably have been not so very different. How in that case were patrons able to meet the demands on their purses?

A small number of very well-to-do patrons might be fortunate enough to have access to funds which were set aside specially for building. At Hereford Cathedral,

Hereford Cathedral: the nave south aisle looking west

for example, the dean and chapter were able to draw on the income from pilgrims visiting the shrine of Saint Thomas de Cantilupe. The prolonged building campaign at the cathedral, inaugurated by Bishop Swinfield at the end of the 1280s, coincided almost exactly with the heyday of Cantilupe's cult and financially was a direct beneficiary of it. According to the fabric roll for 1290–91, of the £286 available for spending that year, no less than £178 came from the tomb of 'the blessed Thomas' and £30 from the alms box.[2] These two items together accounted for nearly two-thirds of the total. The rebuilding, or even part-rebuilding, of a cathedral could consume very considerable amounts of money. The cost of a major reconstruction, such as that undertaken at Exeter or Ely in this period, could work out at between £300 and £700 per bay, depending on the richness of the fabric under construction.[3] At Hereford a decent stretch of Bishop Swinfield's new aisles would probably have consumed the greater part of a single year's income from the visitors and pilgrims. These sums could be afforded by the cathedral when the aspirant saint's cult was at its height; they could not, however, once offerings fell away. In his will, made in 1317, Bishop Swinfield left the sum of 50 marks for the construction of a new chapter house. Significantly, it was not until some 40 years later that the capitular body felt able to embark on the project.

In the case of the lay proprietors who engaged in church building in Herefordshire in this period or, at least, the great majority of them – the gentry class and magnates such as the Mortimers – the costs would have to be met largely from the profits of land. Fortunately for them, this was a time when economic conditions broadly favoured the landlord class and the employers of labour. Until roughly the middle of the century arable prices were high, enabling proprietors to reap a good profit from the produce they sent to market while, at the same time, buoyant population levels assured them not only of a ready labour force but also of healthy rent rolls. In the early fourteenth century labourers' wages were consistently quite modest, varying between roughly 1 1/2d and 2d a day. The cost of raw materials likewise was modest. It was only in the mid 1370s, when prices fell while wages continued to rise, that conditions in the market began to work against the lords. And by then the building boom was over.

Unfortunately, we lack the detailed estate records which would be needed if we were to undertake a full analysis of the income and expenditure of the proprietors who engaged in church building at this time. Just one account roll has come down to us for a manor in knightly ownership, and that is a partial account of Sir Richard de Pembridge's manor of Clehonger, drawn up in 1322 while the property was in royal keeping as a result of its owner's forfeiture.[4] This very summary document records a total income for the half year from March to Michaelmas of £10 10s 0d, a suspiciously low figure which includes few sales of produce and omits the rents of the unfree tenants. A more realistic figure for the value of Sir Richard's property at Clehonger would probably be in the order of £30–£40 per annum.

More helpful are some of the extents, or surveys, of the properties of deceased tenants-in-chief which were drawn up by the escheator and his staff when the tenants' lands were taken into temporary royal keeping.[5] Especially useful is a detailed set of extents drawn up in 1336 on the death of Margaret (d.1334), the long-lived widow of Edmund Mortimer, who was to survive her husband for nearly 30 years and who enjoyed tenure of a substantial share of the family estates.[6] The extents show just how very profitable some of the Mortimers' estates in the Marches could be. An annual value of £34 was placed on Margaret's manor of Eardisland, of £53 on that of Pembridge, £59 on that of Kingsland, £60 on that of Wigmore, and of £59 and £10 respectively on her two Welsh lordships of Radnor and Presteigne. On this evidence, Margaret is likely to have drawn an income each year of between £200 and £300 from her Marcher estates alone, and on top of these she held lands in other counties.[7] If we are correct in supposing that it was Margaret who was responsible for rebuilding the churches of Pembridge and Kingsland, then it is clear that, provided the costs she incurred were spread, she would have had little difficulty in meeting them while still living within her means.

While the buoyancy of income from land in this period can hardly be doubted, it was actually not so much money from rents and crops that fuelled the Herefordshire building boom; it was rather that from another source: the profits of wool. The rich wool clips from the hills of Herefordshire, Shropshire and the Welsh Marches were among the most highly prized in all England. Two main breeds of sheep were reared in England in this period: the first, the tough little sheep which grew short wool and, the second, their larger and fatter counterparts whose wool was longer. The two grades were used for the making of different types of cloth, the long woolled chiefly for lighter worsteds and serges, and the short woolled for heavier texture cloths.[8] The sheep with the long wool were pastured on the rich grasslands of the Cotswolds, East Midlands and Lincolnshire. It was the short-woolled breeds that were reared on the – paradoxically – far poorer pastures of the Welsh Marches; and it was these whose wool was so keenly sought after.

An idea of just how highly prized were the short wools from the Marcher hillsides is afforded by the prices which they fetched. In a schedule compiled in the early fourteenth century, probably between 1318 and 1321, and used by the Italian merchant, Pegolotti, the wool from the two Marcher abbeys of Tintern and Abbey Dore was priced at four times the rate of the lower valued wools – 28 marks a sack as against only seven.[9] This wide price differential is found again in a list of prices fixed for the purveyance of wool for the king's use drawn up in 1337. Prices were fixed county by county, those for Herefordshire coming out top with wool valued at 12 marks per sack, Shropshire next at ten-and-a-half marks, and Lincolnshire third at ten marks. The lowest prices were for wool from the four northernmost counties.[10] The figures fixed in 1337 were lower than those in Pegolotti's list because of the king's natural reluctance to pay premium rates. A second list occasioned by the needs of royal purveyance compiled a few years later in 1343 paints much the same picture, only reversing the order of the top two counties, with Shropshire prices just beating those for Herefordshire.[11] The bulk of the wool clip was bought by middlemen who sent it for export to the great cloth-making cities of Flanders and Italy, where Europe's highest-quality cloths were woven. In the first half of the fourteenth century, when overseas demand was high, there was a remarkable boom in exports, with figures reaching a peak of no fewer than 40,000 sacks a year between 1304 and 1307, before falling back to about 30,000 sacks mid-century under the impact of heavy royal taxation. The result was a substantial surplus on England's balance of payments.

To the great landowners of the Welsh Marches, the wool clips brought massive profits, making possible building projects on a scale which would scarcely otherwise have been imaginable. The Mortimer family especially are likely to have done well for themselves, given that their estates were not only extensive but stretched far into Wales. The scale of their money-making is unfortunately unmeasurable because the clips were disposed of centrally and the accounts have not survived. There can be little doubt, however, that it would have been considerable.[12] Moreover, being bulk producers, the family are likely to have secured higher prices than many of their neighbours. In the circumstances, it is hardly surprising that they were able to pay for wholesale church rebuildings on the scale of those undertaken at Pembridge, Kingsland and elsewhere.

A group equally well placed to benefit financially were the dealers in the local towns to which the clip was brought for sale: dealers, in other words, in such places as Hereford, Leominster and Ludlow. In the late Middle Ages Leominster was so closely associated with the wool trade that the clips brought there came to be known by the name of the town, 'Lemster Ore' – 'ore' because of their golden colour. As Richard Symonds was to write in the 1640s, 'Lemster is famous for fine wool, which makes the finest black and scarlet cloth'.[13] In these circumstances, it is again hardly a matter for surprise that the townsmen of Leominster should have been able to spend so lavishly on building in the heyday of the boom.

If the profits of wool gave the most substantial flock owners the means to build magnificently, it should be remembered that not all the proprietor class were able to benefit equally. The lesser landowners – the gentry and sub-gentry – having smaller estates with less pastureland than their mighty neighbours, were by no means so well placed to profit. Moreover, it is unlikely that they would have been able to accumulate big cash reserves. It is partly for this reason that so few of them undertook complete rebuildings of the kind that the Mortimers undertook at Kingsland and Pembridge. Even the near-total rebuildings which the relatively wealthy Grandisons undertook at Stretton Grandison and Ashperton, were modest by comparison with the Mortimers' commissions. In many cases there is evidence of a search for economy on patrons' part. In Herefordshire, as we have seen, there is a conspicuous absence of liturgical fittings on a scale to compare with those found in Lincolnshire or Nottinghamshire. The only sedilia of any note in the county, those at Leominster and Madley, appear poor relations by comparison with the exuberant examples at Hawton (Notts) or Heckington (Lincs) (*see p. 24*). In Herefordshire, moreover, surface decoration was applied more sparingly than in some parts of England. Ballflower ornament was the county's great speciality, and at Hereford, Leominster and Ledbury its application on window splays makes for displays of enormous richness and intensity. Yet these examples are not characteristic of churches in the county as a whole. Decoration on such a scale was only rarely deployed, and then just on the works of the grandest or wealthiest patrons. By comparison with the churches of south Lincolnshire and the Wash, and even with those of Oxfordshire, many of Herefordshire's churches appear chaste and unadorned.

What is noticeable in Herefordshire and the Marches is that there was a big gap between the very grandest churches, mainly those built in the towns or by the nobility, and the humbler churches built in the countryside by proprietors of more limited means. There is not the broad spectrum of church building that is found in those parts of England where there was a more even distribution of wealth. In Herefordshire a small number of those who commissioned work on parish churches were very rich. The great majority, however, had to watch their pennies. Gentry patrons and clergy rarely indulged in much end-to-end rebuilding of churches.

8

The End of it All

The remarkable period of activity which made Herefordshire one of the most vibrant areas for the production of Decorated architecture was to last for no more than half-a-century. Its beginnings can be traced to the 1290s, when the rebuilding of the cathedral began; its end was to come shortly after the Black Death, when church building everywhere in England ground to a halt. At the cathedral itself the last major work to be undertaken was the vaulting of the new chapter house, finished in about 1370 after some 40 years in the planning. In the diocese the last reasonably well-dated works are the chancel and north chapel at Richard's Castle, the north transept at Ludlow and the north porch at Pembridge. Once these projects were finished, little was accomplished in the county's churches. The Central March's exuberant golden age of Gothic was over.

The reasons for the falling-off in activity are not difficult to find. Essentially, the combination of circumstances which had given rise to the building boom in the first place began to dissolve. The mood of religious enthusiasm, which the cult of St Thomas de Cantilupe had helped to encourage, began to weaken from the 1320s. From around mid-century far fewer perpetual chantries were founded, which in turn meant that fewer chapels were constructed. And, most dramatically of all, the coming of the plague in 1348 sounded the death knell of building because of the loss of large parts of the skilled labour force. Right across England, church building was to be disrupted by the catastrophe of the plague. In Herefordshire and south Shropshire, however, in contrast to some other areas, there was to be no subsequent recovery.

In the diocese, it was the rise and fall of the cult of Hereford's local saint, Thomas de Cantilupe, that did most to determine the chronology of the building boom. For a generation or more, the upsurge in building and the fortunes of the saint's cult had gone together, the one lending strength to the other. At the height of the cult, the offerings made by pilgrims visiting the saint's shrine yielded huge sums for the cathedral fabric fund. In 1290–91 no less than £178 10s 7d was received at the offerings

Hereford Cathedral: the central tower from the north-west

box: roughly two-thirds of the total sum spent on building that year. In 1307, when a papal commission of enquiry was appointed to look into the case for Cantilupe's canonisation, offerings were still described as 'bountiful', and it was reported that legacies were being received too.[1] The building of the new central tower was largely paid for from pilgrims' offerings. By 1320, however, the year in which canonisation was finally conceded, receipts at the shrine were already moving into decline. All medieval saints' cults were apt to be meteor-like, rising and falling very quickly. Even St Thomas Becket's shrine at Canterbury, the most prestigious in England, experienced a late medieval falling-off in popularity, with receipts, which had totalled over £1,000 in 1220, shrinking to less than £100 by the early sixteenth century. At

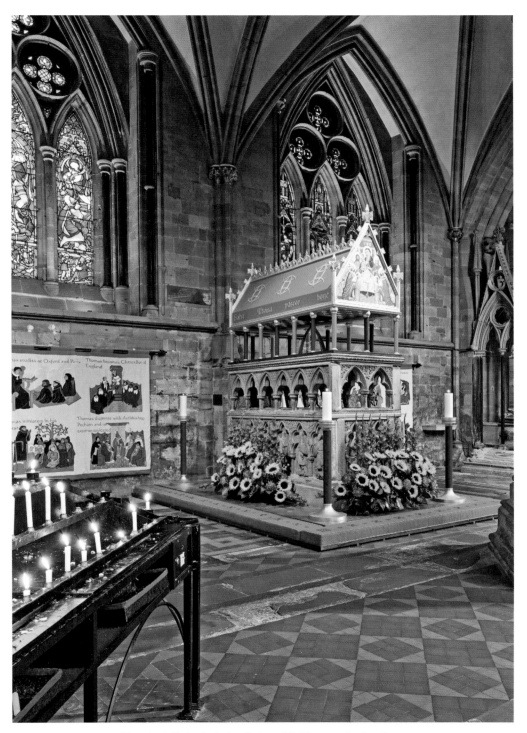

Hereford Cathedral: the shrine of St Thomas de Cantilupe

Hereford, St Thomas de Cantilupe's cult was producing a mere £2 13s 4d by 1383, the next year for which we have accounts.[2] By the end of the fourteenth century the tide of personal religious enthusiasm in England was anyway flowing in new and very different channels. Walsingham in Norfolk, a focus of Marian devotion, was becoming the fashionable place for pilgrims to visit. Hereford, with its saint of more local appeal, was becoming something of a backwater.

The slackening of religious enthusiasm quickly showed in the slowing of building work at the cathedral. After the 1310s money was in shorter supply than before. By 1319, when repairs were needed to the central tower, the dean and chapter had to appeal to the pope for financial assistance; they were unable to afford to meet the costs themselves. With the gradual winding down of building activity from 1320, the cathedral masons' lodge inevitably began to lose men. Highly skilled craftsmen, who had been drawn to the cathedral by the prospect of good work and regular wages, now moved elsewhere. No longer could a patron in the vicinity of Hereford, minded to rebuild or add to a parish church, think of calling on the services of a mason from the cathedral yard. From now on, such a person would have to go in search elsewhere. The men who undertook the works at Kingsland, Ludlow and Richard's Castle in the 1340s and 1350s appear to have been drawn from places as far afield as Worcester, Lichfield and Bristol. The tie between the cathedral and the diocese, which for so long had been crucial not only to the dissemination of St Thomas de Cantilupe's cult but also to the carrying out of the building and glazing schemes closely linked with it, now began to loosen and eventually dissolve. The ending of this tie goes a long way to explaining why the pace of church building in Herefordshire slowed so sharply from mid-century.

If there was a link between the building boom and the fortunes of Thomas de Cantilupe's cult, so likewise was there one between the pace of building activity and the chronology of perpetual chantry foundations in this period. On the evidence of the licences for alienation of land into mortmain, no fewer than 934 chantries were established in England between 1299 and 1348, the highest number for any half-century in the Middle Ages.[3] In Herefordshire alone some two-dozen foundations are known to have been established, and there were almost certainly many more. A number of these were accommodated in purpose-built side aisles or chapels. Good examples of such structures are to be seen at Clehonger, Westhide, Dilwyn and King's Pyon. The huge aisle at Westhide is one of the most striking creations of the Decorated period in the county (*see p. 59*).[4] In the second half of the century, however, far fewer perpetual chantry foundations were to be established than before. Nationally, again on the evidence of the licences, there were some 670 foundations between 1350 and 1399, and only 290 in the half-century after that. Accordingly, the drive for the construction of new chapels rapidly slowed from about 1350. Herefordshire Decorated, as we have seen, was to find its characteristic expression not so much in whole churches but in additions to churches. Most of these date from the years between 1300 and 1350. The north chapel at Richard's Castle, which dates from the 1350s, is one of the last.

By the time the heyday of perpetual chantry foundations was passing, the social and economic scene had anyway been transformed. In the summer and winter of 1348–49 the Black Death swept across England, claiming the lives of some 2–3 million people. England's population on the eve of the visitation probably stood somewhere in the order of 6 million or so. By the time the scourge had passed, it had fallen to no more than 4 million, and subsequent plague visitations were to reduce it further still. The impact on life in Herefordshire and south Shropshire can be traced in the records of the diocese of Hereford. In just four episcopal manors – those of Bosbury, Colwall, Coddington and Cradley, along the eastern border of the diocese – as many as 158 tenants are reported to have been carried away. Further north, at Great and Little Collington, the incidence of mortality among both parishioners and clergy was such that by 1352 it was necessary to merge the two parishes.[5] Among the clergy, who by virtue of their work were brought into regular contact with the dead and dying, the rate of mortality was especially severe. Of the more than 300 benefices in the diocese, well over half lost their incumbent during the 12 months of the plague. A number of these were the result of resignations or exchanges. The great majority, however, resulted from the death of the previous incumbent. In 1348 there had been just 11 institutions to benefices in the diocese. In 1349 there were as many as 160.[6]

The effect of the fall in population on landlord incomes was, perhaps surprisingly, by no means immediate. Although labourers' wages rose sharply in the wake of the plague, prices of agricultural produce were for a while to remain correspondingly buoyant, enabling employers to more than cover their costs. Only in the mid-1370s, after further plague visitations, were prices to fall dramatically, and they were then to remain low, except in years of dearth, for the rest of the Middle Ages. Landlords did their best to maintain the levels of income from their estates by a mixture of flexibility, cajolery and resourcefulness. Where tenements were standing empty for lack of tenants, they resorted to engrossment: that is to say, they allowed other tenants to add them to their own lands for an increase in rent. At Dilwyn, the lord was able to maintain a full rent roll into at least the 1380s by this means.[7] As for demesne agriculture, in many cases lords switched from arable to pastoral husbandry, a far less labour-intensive form of activity than its counterpart. Inevitably, however, arrears are still found building up on accounts. At the twin manors of Presteigne and Norton, which belonged to the Mortimers, in 1383–84 arrears amounted to at least half the income for which the local bailiff was nominally held liable, and at Wigmore to as much as two-thirds.[8] These are much higher figures than can be explained in terms of cash-in-hand held by the bailiff. What hit landlords especially hard in these years was a substantial collapse in income from leases and the profits of jurisdiction: tenants, aware of their new bargaining power, were simply refusing to pay.[9] By the end of the fourteenth century lords who had not been able to add to their properties, had considerably less spending power at their disposal than they had once had. And this in turn meant that they had less money to spend on church building. To add to their woes, the rise in the cost of skilled labour after 1350 likewise counted against them. In the pre-Black Death period the wages of building labourers had been reasonably low.[10] By half-a-century later they were much higher. For many, church building was in danger of becoming unaffordable.

Right across England there was a sharp downturn in the number of building starts in the years after the Black Death. The period from around 1250 to 1300 had been an intensely active one in church building, and the half-century that followed hardly less so. The half-century after the Black Death, however, was to be very different. By 1400 there were only about half the number of major church-building projects under way that there had been a century earlier, and the number of lesser projects is likely to have been much the same.[11] There were a number of reasons for this unprecedented downturn, among them the need to consolidate resources and the competition for patrons' favour from the friars. But the sheer unaffordability of building was probably the most important factor of all.

In those areas of England where there were large sheep flocks, income from the sale of wool offered hard-pressed landowners a measure of relief. Although in the late fourteenth century the trend of wool exports was broadly downward, in consequence of the imposition of royal taxation, there were still years when sales were good, and prices remained buoyant. In the fifteenth century high demand for the very finest wools caused these to maintain or even increase their value. In 1454 Hereford wool was priced at 19½ marks, higher even than it had been in the 1340s, and Leominster and Shropshire wool fetched prices at least the equal of those a century before.[12] It is possible that the middle of the fifteenth century was an exceptional time, however, and that in other years prices were lower. In the absence of more evidence for wool prices in the March, it is very difficult for us to tell. But what cannot be gainsaid is that in volume terms sales of wool to the big Flemish or Italian buyers were in long-term decline.

In some parts of England the decline in sales to exporters was at least partly offset by a corresponding increase in sales to domestic buyers, who themselves made the wool into cloth. In East Anglia and parts of Wiltshire, Somerset and Devon the domestic cloth industry was booming, protected by the tariff wall afforded by the tax on exports. This shift in the pattern of trade to domestic manufacture, however, did little to assist growers in Herefordshire and the Marches. The types of cloth in which the East Anglian manufacturers chose to specialise were the lighter, coarser fabrics, notably the cheap worsteds, which sold widely across England. But these were fabrics made from the wools of northern England, Romney Marsh and the Midlands, not from the prize Herefordshire or Shropshire fleeces. By default, the proprietors of the Marches found themselves reliant principally on sales to exporters. And, hit by the heavy burden of royal taxation, these were in freefall in the second half of the century.

In the parts of England, principally the eastern counties, where the rural cloth industry took root, there was a corresponding revival of church building in the fifteenth century. In Norfolk and Suffolk almost every church was either wholly or partly rebuilt in the years between 1400 and the Reformation. The story was much the same in Devon and Somerset. Fifteenth-century church building was the product of a redistribution of wealth from the lords to a more broadly-based proprietor class that included small-scale growers and rural cloth-manufacturers. It was a corporate activity, one that in the larger parishes involved perhaps dozens of participants. The patronage of church building in the Decorated period, at least in Herefordshire and the Marches, had been altogether different. Building had been carried on principally by the lordly class, the nobility and gentry, the cathedral clergy, the founders of chantry chapels, and the wealthy townsmen. These are the people we see represented in the donor panels they commissioned in their stained glass windows or on the tomb monuments which they installed in their chantry chapels. Building in the Decorated style, partly because of the style's ornateness, was mainly an elite activity. It required money. It was not something easily done through communal patronage. Nor was it something that could be carried on in straitened economic circumstances.

Largely because there was little rural cloth-making in Herefordshire and the Marches, there was little Perpendicular church building. Perpendicular churches in the Marches are remarkably few. The grandest and best-known example is the parish church at Ludlow, a town which most definitely did flourish in the fifteenth century. The magnificent central tower, dating from the third quarter of the century, which dominates the structure, is a landmark for miles around. So extensive was the fifteenth-century rebuilding at Ludlow that it is easy to overlook the fact that important Decorated work is to be seen in the remarkable hexagonal porch, the north aisle of the nave, and the transepts. Just two complete Perpendicular churches are to be found in the Marches, both in Shropshire and both of medium size. One is the collegiate

Tong church

church at Tong, paid for by Isabel Pembridge and begun in 1410, and the other is Henry IV's Battlefield memorial chapel near Shrewsbury. Elsewhere, Perpendicular work is confined mostly to parts of buildings or to micro-architecture. Good examples are afforded by the west window of Shrewsbury Abbey, the south porch at Ballingham (Heref.) and the south transept vault, Stanbury chapel and outer north porch at Hereford Cathedral. Surprisingly, there was to be no building in the Perpendicular period at Leominster, another town which did well in the late Middle Ages.

The absence of any large-scale Perpendicular architecture inevitably means that Herefordshire and the Marches are lacking in the magnificent glasshouse churches which grace the East Anglian landscape. All is not lost, however. A by-product of the fifteenth-century dearth is that the Marches are not deprived of their rich heritage of Decorated architecture, architecture of a sort rarely encountered in East Anglia. In England's rich and varied landscape, most regions or counties have their own local architectural speciality. In Herefordshire and south Shropshire in the twelfth century it is Romanesque. In the fourteenth, it is Decorated.

GAZETTEER

There are only a handful of complete Decorated churches in Herefordshire and the area of the central March, all of them small. Decorated work is found more characteristically in piecemeal additions to fabrics – an aisle added here, a side chapel there – or in the re-fenestration and reglazing of existing fabrics. What follows is a list of those churches in the central March in which the most exciting Decorated work is to be found, with a few notes on the history and artistic or architectural distinction of each. After this, there is a second list, of churches of lesser importance, which nonetheless still have features that make them well worth a visit. All the churches are in Herefordshire unless otherwise indicated.

CREDENHILL

A church with a gem of a stained glass window: a tiny panel on the south side of the chancel showing two bishops standing next to each other in the act of blessing (*see p. 64*). On the left is England's martyr saint, Thomas Becket, identifiable from his pallium and cross-staff, and on the right his namesake, Thomas de Cantilupe of Hereford, shown with a crozier. The quality of the glass is superb. The colours are predominantly blue, green and ruby on the vestments, and there are golden castles and fleurs-de-lis on blue and ruby grounds in the borders. What is remarkable is that the two episcopal icons should be shown next to each other, so as to emphasise the parallels between them. On stylistic grounds, the window can be dated to the first decade of the century, sometime before Cantilupe's canonisation in 1320. In other words, it was almost certainly conceived as part of an unofficial campaign to promote Cantilupe's cause, and was designed to encourage onlookers to regard the bishop in some sense as Becket's equal. The man responsible for the commission was probably Philip Talbot, a canon of Hereford Cathedral and member of an important local gentry family, who had been instituted into Credenhill church by Cantilupe and who founded a chantry there in 1306.

Eaton Bishop

The chief glory here is the chancel east window, which has some of Herefordshire's finest fourteenth-century stained glass (*see p. 25 & p. 69*). In its present form, which may not entirely correspond to the original, the scheme consists of, in the centre and from left to right, the Virgin and Child, St Michael, a bishop, St Gabriel and a reset head of Christ, all under tall canopies, a Crucifixion above the bishop, and a series of donor figures along the bottom. The handling of the Virgin and Child, with the Christ Child fondling his mother's chin, is especially sensitive. Typical of the glass of this period is the trellis decoration behind the figures or scenes, here yellow on blue for the Crucifixion, and red on green for the two Archangels. Some of the glass has affinities with glass of the same period at Moccas and Madley (Heref.), Ludlow (Salop), and in the choir clerestory at Tewkesbury, and the work of a single workshop may be suspected. The identity of the tonsured figures along the bottom is in some cases uncertain, as the inscriptions are incomplete and may not all be in their original positions. What is clear, however, is that the central figure in academic robes, identified as 'Magister A … uth Cantor', is Adam Murimuth DCL, the chronicler, a canon of Hereford, later a canon of Exeter, who is known to have become cantor of Exeter in 1328. The figure on the left is identified in the inscription as one John Kent, another clerk, and it is suggested that the figure on the right is Murimuth's mother. Adam Murimuth has no recorded connection with Eaton Bishop, but was presumably one of a group of clerics who contributed to the cost of the window. The living of Eaton Bishop was in the gift of the bishops of Hereford.

Hereford Cathedral

Although at its core a wholly Romanesque building, Hereford Cathedral presents externally a completely Gothic aspect, the product of a major late thirteenth- and early fourteenth-century remodelling (*see pp. 28–29*). The spur to the new work was the cult of Hereford's saint, Thomas de Cantilupe, bishop from 1275 to 1282, which both prompted the need for a grander cathedral and provided the financial wherewithal to bring this about. West of the choir, the only post-Romanesque part of the fabric which predates the remodelling is the north transept, a remarkable structure raised by Bishop Pierre d'Aigueblanche in the 1260s in the style of

Tomb of Bishop d'Aigueblanche

Westminster Abbey. The main remodelling was initiated by Bishop Swinfield in the 1290s and involved turning the aisles of both choir and nave into a grand processional way to the east end, where Cantilupe, once canonised, was to be buried. As soon as the aisles were finished, two new eastern transepts were built, the northern one conceived by Bishop Swinfield as a burial place for himself and his family. Externally, the dominant feature is the central tower, a big two-storey structure heavily ornamented, and loaded with thousands of ballflowers. Stylistically the tower was to be one of the models for its slightly later and more slender cousin, the tower of Salisbury Cathedral. The tower over the west front was likewise rebuilt, but is now lost. A notable feature of the interior is the long sequence of retrospective episcopal effigies in both north and south choir aisles, a product of Bishop Swinfield's desire to attest to the antiquity of the see of Hereford (*see p. 44*).

KINGSLAND

Kingsland is a church which owes its distinction in part to the presence nearby of a Mortimer residence, in this case a castle, the earthworks of which still remain. The building was probably paid for by Margaret (d.1334), the long-lived widow of Edmund, Lord Mortimer, and initiated shortly before her death. The design is a simple but elegant one. The five-bay nave has tall arcades with shafted piers which have a late-Gothic feel, arches which are only gently pointed, and 'porthole' windows over the spandrels, not the apexes. The architect of the church was clearly someone familiar with the styles of the Bristol workshops and may actually have come from Bristol. What

Fourteenth-century glass in the east window at Kingsland

indicates this is the polygonal door-heads which he used instead of conventional arches, a motif derived from the tomb recesses in St Augustine's Abbey, Bristol (now Bristol Cathedral) (*see p. 42*). A curiosity of the church is the lean-to Volka chapel, built into the angle between the north aisle of the nave and the north porch. This is a tiny space, evidently intended as a chantry, with an east window of four lights and an unusual north window of six straight-headed lights above and three big square ones below (*see p. 82*). On the south side of the chapel is a tomb recess which has been associated with Walter Mortimer, an incumbent of the church in the 1320s. A rare survival is the original fourteenth-century sacristy on the north side of the chancel.

Ledbury

A large town church with a detached tower and spire, the main part of the building predominantly of the late thirteenth- and early fourteenth-centuries. From the outside, the long south aisle frontage presents a fine sight, with its symmetrical buttressing and row of eight big windows, all of the stepped lancet type but with heads differing in detail.

The north chapel at Ledbury – east elevation window tracery

The gem of the building is the outer north chapel, a show-piece of Herefordshire Decorated and a tour de force by any standard. It is a big rectangular structure, illuminated by five four-light windows, two along each side and one in the end wall, all with intricate tracery and encrusted with ballflower both inside and out. Access to the chapel was through a door in the south-west angle, which is again richly decorated, in this case by rows of fleurons. The chapel can be dated on stylistic grounds to around 1330 and was probably the work of a mason who had worked at either Hereford Cathedral or Tewkesbury Abbey, or both. Around the corner from it, in the chapel at the end of the north aisle, is the fine tomb monument of a lady of the Pauncefot family, which follows the slightly earlier monument of Lady Grandison at Much Marcle in showing the lady's dress falling naturalistically over the side of the chest (*see p. 51*).

Leominster Priory

Leominster Priory was an ancient foundation, a former Anglo-Saxon minster church re-established in the 1120s by King Henry I as a cell of his newly-founded abbey at Reading. The western half of the former conventual church was acquired by the townsfolk at the Reformation for use as their parish church. The bulk of the fabric as we have it is severe Romanesque, a central vessel, ending in a later tower, flanked by a north and south aisle. In the thirteenth century a fourth aisle was added to the south, to provide the townsfolk with worshipping space of their own, separate from that of the monks. In the early fourteenth century this aisle was rebuilt on an opulent scale, to provide one of the show-pieces of Herefordshire Decorated. Best appreciated from the south-west, on the approach to the porch, this magnificent structure has a west window and a row of five windows on the south side, all of four lights, tall and wide, and studded with ballflower. The impression is one of extreme richness. The complex tracery design stands somewhere between that of the Hereford Cathedral central tower and the south aisle of Gloucester. Almost certainly the architect responsible for the aisle was a mason who had worked at Hereford.

The south aisle at Leominster – two of the five south elevation windows

Little Hereford

An atmospheric church set on the banks of the Teme, surrounded by the earthworks of the former village, the present-day hamlet of Little Hereford lying mainly to the north of the main road. Immediately to the south-east of the church is the triangular platform of a small motte-and-bailey castle probably thrown up in the civil war of King Stephen's reign. The church is a simple one, consisting of an aisleless nave and chancel and a solid keep-like west tower with a pyramidal roof. The bulk of the fabric dates from the thirteenth century, but in the early fourteenth the chancel was enlarged to accommodate the burials of the de la Mare family, the lords of the manor. Against the north wall are two fine, conjoined tomb recesses, both canopied and with ogee gables, the eastern one containing a remarkable survival, the incised slab of a lady of the de la Mare family. The tiny chancel arch, probably contemporary with the lengthening, reinforces the character of the chancel as a private space, the preserve of the lord of the manor (*see p. 89*). In the nave is a slightly earlier canopied tomb recess, which may be the burial place of Sir John de la Mare, knight of the shire for Herefordshire in the parliament of 1298. A later member of the family, Sir Peter, steward of the earl of March, was the first Speaker of the House of Commons, serving in that capacity in the 'Good' Parliament of 1376.

LUDLOW, ST LAURENCE (SALOP)
A grand, mainly fifteenth-century church, but with a nave north aisle, south porch and transepts all of the early fourteenth century. The porch is hexagonal, like its counterpart at St Mary Redcliffe, Bristol, which is of about the same date, and the influence of Bristol masons may be detected. The north aisle windows are all richly adorned with ballflower, best appreciated from the outside (*p. 38*). Inside, note the elaborate tomb recess in the north aisle, probably the burial place of a member of the Verdon family, who helped pay for the aisle.

MADLEY
A giant of a church, rather aloof in its grandeur, and all the more memorable for standing in so tiny a village. In the Middle Ages it was the subject of considerable pilgrim interest because of its possession of an image of the Virgin Mary, which was the focus of a cult. The living was a valuable one, worth £43 a year, and from 1219 it was in the possession of the dean and chapter of Hereford.

The oldest part of the church is the north porch, which was probably the north transept of the pre-Gothic church. This early building was transformed in the thirteenth century in a major remodelling which gave us the present sturdy west tower and the long, six-bay nave which, at the west end, wraps around the tower. No sooner was this remodelling complete than another great campaign was initiated (c.1310), probably in response to a boom in the popularity of the Marian image. A magnificent new chancel was built with a remarkable polygonal apse and, below it, a vaulted crypt, in which presumably the image was housed, and access to which was gained by stairs on both the north and the south sides. This building campaign was brought to an end in the 1330s with the construction of the Chilston chapel, in the form of an outer south aisle, probably to accommodate a chantry foundation for the benefit of the Dunre and Swinfield families (*see pp. 73–74*). There are remains of a once high-quality glazing scheme in the windows of the apse.

Madley church. *Left*: detail of the arcade of the Chilston aisle, showing ballflower-decorated capital.
Right: thirteenth- and fourteenth-century glass in the chancel east window

PEMBRIDGE

The grandeur of this church owes much to the village's importance as the site of a flourishing market, and the presence, to the south of the churchyard, of a castle used by the Mortimers as a dower property. Apart from the detached belfry and two blocked-up thirteenth-century arches in the chancel, the fabric belongs entirely to the fourteenth century, everything to the west of the chancel apparently the product of a four or five-year rebuilding campaign begun around 1330. The patron responsible for the work was almost certainly Margaret (d.1334), the long-lived widow of Edmund, Lord Mortimer, and mother of Roger, the first earl.

The plan of the church is ambitious, even cathedralesque, comprising a long chancel, north and south transepts, and a spacious six-bay nave with clerestory and aisles (*see pp. 39, 76 & 80*). As at Kingsland, a distinctive feature of the clerestory is the use of circular windows with cinquefoils, placed over the

Pembridge church: the nave arcade

spandrels and not the apexes of the arches. In the absence of the usual west tower, the west façade provides something of a show front, its dominant feature a large four-light window with reticulated tracery. The main entrance is through the north porch, an addition made later in the century. Inside, the tall nave arcades convey an impression of height, while the view east is enhanced by the lateral expansion at the crossing into the transepts. In the chancel, on a restored tomb chest, are two pairs of effigies commemorating Nicholas Gour and his wife and their son John and his own wife. Nicholas is shown in the attire of a serjeant-at-law, or pleader in the central courts, and his son, with his puffed hat, in that of an attorney or solicitor (*see p. 53*). The Gours were lords of Marston in the parish of Pembridge and were associates of the Mortimers, John serving Earl Roger (d.1360) as his steward and then as keeper of his estates after his death. The two monuments provide superb examples of the medieval tomb sculptor's art.

Richard's Castle

An evocative church, now redundant, standing in what was once the outer bailey of the castle, commanding wide views over the plain to the east. The relative size of the building is explained by the fact that Richard's Castle was a borough from 1086 and was the site of a market and fair from 1216. From the outside, the building looks squat and irregular, mellow in its pale red sandstone, and unusual for having a detached bell tower – in this case, off to the east, away from the castle. Inside, it is a building that comes across as loveable, pleasantly unrestored, the nave arcade held up by broad wooden struts with huge screw threads.

The core of the nave, which is broad, is twelfth-century Romanesque. In the early fourteenth century an aisle was added to the south in order to accommodate a chantry founded by Joan, daughter and co-heiress of Hugh de Mortimer, the last of his line (*see overleaf*). Its east window is studded externally with ballflower, and there is also ballflower on the capitals of the low pillars. In the 1350s or early 1360s the chancel was rebuilt and extended, and a magnificent curvilinear window inserted in the east wall, while on the north side of the nave a projecting chapel was added, again presumably to accommodate a chantry. Separating the chapel from the nave is a two-bay arcade, the columns and responds of which are crowned by castellated capitals with fleuron decoration. These later works were probably undertaken on the initiative of Sir John Talbot, Joan's son by her second marriage to Sir Richard Talbot of Goodrich. Fragments of medieval stained glass survive in the windows of the south aisle and the north chapel.

STRETFORD

A small rubblestone building, almost as wide as it is long, set at the end of a cul-de-sac with only a farm for company; the village has largely disappeared. The development of the fabric is complex. The original nave and chancel appear to have been what are today the north aisle and chapel, these being essentially twelfth-century work. In the thirteenth century the existing nave and chancel were added to the south, and a low, three-bay arcade constructed between the two sections. In the early fourteenth century the whole structure was lengthened some eight feet to the east, and finally, in about 1540, a new timber roof raised over the two vessels, legible externally today as a single gabled roof covering the whole fabric. The chief delight of the interior is found in the two locally produced sandstone monuments in the north aisle and chapel commemorating two successive generations of the de la Bere family and their wives. The monuments are so alike that they must have been commissioned at the same time – on the evidence of the armour probably in the late 1340s. The monument under the crude arch in the aisle, which shows slightly more developed armour, probably commemorates Sir John de la Bere, who must have commissioned the monuments, and his wife, Agnes, and that in the chapel, his parents, Sir Robert and his wife (*see p. 49*). Both monuments are in curiously shallow relief, perhaps because they were cut from a narrow vein of stone. The de la Beres were a widely ramified family with branches not only in Herefordshire but in Berkshire and South Wales. The Herefordshire branch were closely allied to the Mortimers.

WEOBLEY

The church stands a little apart from the pretty black-and-white former market town to its south, and is dominated by its spectacular north-west tower and spire (*see p. 126*). The greater part of the fabric – nave, chancel and north transept – designed by a mason who had worked at the cathedral, is the product of a rebuilding which proceeded in stages, and drew to a close in about 1325. The nave with its characteristic octagonal piers was probably the architectural model for that at Pembridge. On the west door there is a splendid display of ballflower (*see p. 17*).

Overleaf: Richard's Castle church: the south aisle and double-chamfered nave arcade with ballflower capitals (note the bracing struts between the arcade and the south wall, at top left)

The best of the rest

ALLENSMORE

A small aisleless church mainly of the early fourteenth century, with good examples of the Y-shaped window tracery characteristic of Herefordshire Decorated (*see p. 14*). In the chancel is the superb incised and colour-filled inlay slab of Sir Andrew Herley (d.1392) and his wife, showing the couple under a double canopy (*see p. 53*). In the 1340s Allensmore was the scene of a tussle over churchyard burial rights between the dean of Hereford, who claimed to a monopoly of burials for the cathedral, and the villagers, led by the lady of the manor, who wanted a local burial place of their own. In the end the villagers won.

BODENHAM

Although built by a family – the Devereux – who had sunk from the baronage to the knightly class by the fourteenth century, Bodenham is a big church, tall and airy inside. In the chancel is the beautiful tomb monument, dating from about 1300, of a Devereux lady with a child by her side sheltered in the robes of her dress (*see p. 48*).

CHELMARSH (SALOP)

A rare example of a complete small Decorated church, paid for in all probability by Sir Hugh Mortimer, lord of Chelmarsh, who founded a chantry in the church in 1345 (*see p. 30*). The building, probably designed by a mason who had also worked at Stottesdon, is a modest one, consisting of a west tower (in its present form dating from 1720), a nave and chancel under one roof and a north aisle. Inside, the widely-spaced ballflower on the capitals should be noted. Strangely, there is no founder's monument in the church.

DILWYN

The curiosity of the church is the way in which the south arcade of the nave crashes awkwardly into the middle of the tower arch, while the north arcade is offset to the right. Evidently the position of the main part of the church was shifted to the north when the church was rebuilt in the late thirteenth century. The church is a rich and varied one. It has a good tomb effigy in the chancel and a selection of cross slab grave covers at the west end (*see pp. 41 & 93*).

KING'S PYON

The outstanding feature is the splendid early fourteenth-century roofs over the nave and transept. That over the nave is of four bays with cambered tie beams, foiled struts to the principals and trefoiled braces below the collar, supported along the sides by braces formed of two ranges of trefoiled arches (*see p. 90*). The overall effect is overwhelming.

MARDEN

The church, which stands away from the village by the River Lugg, is notable for one impressive feature, a chancel ending in a polygonal apse in the manner of Madley (*see p. 38*). The similarity of the window tracery to that at Leominster Priory points to the involvement of a Leominster-trained mason. The nave and aisles were rebuilt in the nineteenth century.

MUCH MARCLE

A large fourteenth-century church notable especially for the magnificent tomb monument of Blanche, Lady Grandison (*see p. 51*), and for the wooden effigy, likewise fourteenth-century, of a civilian, probably a member of the Helyon family.

ROSS-ON-WYE

A large, if heavily restored, town church with an early fourteenth-century tower and a rebuilt spire that dominate the view from across the Wye. The body of the church is thirteenth- and early fourteenth-century work, and the airy interior conveys a sense of spaciousness, which is characteristic of the more ambitious Decorated churches (*see p. 19*). Today, Ross is distinguished principally for its fine collection of sixteenth-century and later monuments, the grander of them to the Rudhall family, who lived nearby.

Ross church: piscina with ballflower

WESTHIDE

A small church dominated on the approach side by the massive south chapel, built about 1340 to accommodate a chantry by an unidentified patron whose tomb effigy is in a recess in the south wall (*see p. 59*). The patron entered the church by the main south door, to which a porch was later added, while the parishioners' entrance was by a much smaller door tucked in the south-west angle by the tower. Inside the church, the chancel arch is placed off-centre to permit a view of the high altar from the south chapel. There are traces of original paintwork on the arch of the tomb recess and the soffit of the east window. By the east window are two fine head-stops.

Weobley church: detail of the north-west tower, showing the corner pinnacles and lucarnes

GLOSSARY

BALLFLOWER	A decorative device in the form of three leaves opening up to reveal a small ball, generally found in the hollow of a moulding
CAPITAL	The head of a column
CINQUEFOIL	A form of architectural decoration in the shape of a five-lobed leaf
CLERESTORY	The uppermost storey in the elevation of a church, generally pierced by windows
CURVILINEAR	A form of window tracery with uninterrupted flowing curves
FILLET	A narrow, flat band of stone running down a shaft alongside a moulding
GEOMETRICAL	A form of window tracery consisting of circular openings in the head, typically two circles above the main lights and a third at the point of the arch
LANCET	A slender, single-light pointed arch window
LUCARNE	A window-like opening in a spire, generally small and gabled
MOUCHETTE	In window tracery, a shape like a dagger but with curved sides
MOULDING	A shaped ornamental strip of continuous section, e.g. on an arch or window surround
MULLION	The vertical shaft of stone between the lights of a window
OCULUS	A circular opening, a form often employed in Decorated window tracery
OGEE	The double curve of an arch, bending first one way and then the other
RETICULATED	In window tracery, a net-like pattern of ogee-ended lozenges
SEXFOIL	A form of architectural decoration in the form of a six-lobed leaf
SOFFIT	The underside of an arch
SPANDREL	The roughly triangular space either between an arch and its containing rectangle or between arches
TRANSEPT	The transverse arm of a church
TREFOIL	A form of architectural decoration in the shape of a three lobed-leaf. A pointed trefoil is one in which the lobes are sharply pointed
TRIFORIUM	The middle storey in the elevation of a medieval church

SELECT BIBLIOGRAPHY

UNPRINTED SOURCES

British Library, London

Additional MS 17458	notes of David Powell
Egerton Roll 8362	account roll of the manor and banlieu of Wigmore
Harley MS 944	Richard Symonds's notebook
Harley MS 1240	Mortimer family cartulary
Harley MS 6726	Notes of Silas Taylor

Herefordshire Archives and Records Centre, Hereford

A31/25	account roll of the honor of Wigmore
F78/1/5	rental of the manor of Dilwyn

The National Archives, Kew

C135/45/22	inquisition post mortem of Margaret Mortimer
SC6/1145/16	account roll of the manor of Clehonger

PRINTED SOURCES

Bannister, A.T. (ed.), *Registrum Ade de Orleton, Episcopi Herefordensis, A.D. MCCCXVII–MCCCXXVII* (Canterbury and York Society, 5, 1908)

Calendar of Close Rolls 1301–1399 (25 vols., London: HMSO, 1892–1927)

Calendar of Inquisitions Post Mortem 1300–77 (11 vols., London: HMSO, 1913–52)

Calendar of Patent Rolls 1301–1399 (28 vols., London: HMSO, 1894–1909)

Capes, W.W. (ed.), *Charters and Records of Hereford Cathedral* (Hereford, 1908)

— *Registrum Ricardi de Swinfield, Episcopi Herefordensis, A.D. MCCLXXXIII–MCCCXVII* (Canterbury and York Society, 6, 1909)

— *Registrum Thome de Cantilupo, Episcopi Herefordensis, A.D. MCCLXXV–MCCLXXXII* (Canterbury and York Society, 2, 1907)

Dingley, T., *History from Marble*, ed. T.E. Winnington (Camden Society, old series 97, 1868)

Feudal Aids, 1284–1431, 6 vols. (London, 1899–1920)

Le Neve, J., *Fasti Ecclesiae Anglicanae, 1300–1541, II, Hereford Diocese*, ed. J.M. Horn (London, 1962)

Long, C.E. (ed.), *Richard Symonds's Diary of the Marches of the Royal Army* (Camden Society, old series 74 (1859)

Remfrey, P.M. (ed.), *The Wigmore Chronicle, 1066–1377* (Shrewsbury, 2013)

SECONDARY SOURCES

Aston, K., and Klein, P., *A Walk around the church of St Mary the Virgin, Pembridge, Herefordshire* (Pembridge, 2005)

Aylmer, G., and Tiller, J. (eds.), *Hereford Cathedral. A History* (London, 2000)

Bass, I.L., 'Miraculous Marches: the cult of Thomas de Cantilupe and the Mortimers', *Journal of the Mortimer History Society*, 1 (2017)
— 'Miracle in the Marches', *History Today*, 67, 3 (2017)

Biebrach, R., *Church Monuments in South Wales, c.1200–1547* (Woodbridge, 2017)

Binski, P., *Gothic Wonder. Art, Artifice and the Decorated Style, 1290–1350* (New Haven and London, 2014)

Brooks, A., and Pevsner, N., *Herefordshire* (New Haven and London, 2012)

Cokayne, G.E., and others, *The Complete Peerage*, St Catherine's Press, 12 vols. in 13, (London, 1910–57)

Coldstream, N., *The Decorated Style. Architecture and Ornament, 1240–1360* (London, 1994)

Davies, R.R., *Lordship and Society in the March of Wales, 1282–1400* (Oxford, 1978)

Dohar, W.J., *The Black Death and Pastoral Leadership. The Diocese of Hereford in the Fourteenth Century* (Philadelphia, 1995)

Emden, A.B., *A Biographical Register of the University of Oxford to A.D. 1500*, 3 vols., (Oxford, 1957–59)

Gittos, B. and M., *The Tomb of Blanche Mortimer, Lady Grandisson at Much Marcle* (Much Marcle, 2017)

Hillaby, J. and C., *Leominster Minster, Priory and Borough, c.660–1539* (Almeley, 2006)

Holmes, G.A., *The Estates of the Higher Nobility in Fourteenth-Century England* (Cambridge, 1957)

Hopkinson, G., 'The Mortimers of Wigmore, 1282–1330', *Transactions of the Woolhope Naturalists' Field Club*, 48 (1995)

Hume, P., *On the Trail of the Mortimers* (Almeley, 2016)

Jancey, M. (ed.), *St Thomas Cantilupe, Bishop of Hereford. Essays in his Honour* (Hereford, 1982)

Lloyd, T.H., *The Movement of Wool Prices in Medieval England* (Cambridge: *Economic History Review Supplement*, 6, 1973)

Marshall, G., 'Some remarks on the ancient stained glass in Eaton Bishop church, co. Hereford', *Transactions of the Woolhope Naturalists' Field Club*, 24 (1922)

— 'The church of Richard's Castle, co. Hereford', *Transactions of the Woolhope Naturalists' Field Club*, 25 (1924–26)

— 'Notes on Kingsland church', *Transactions of the Woolhope Naturalists' Field Club*, 27 (1930–32)

— 'Stretford church, co. Hereford', *Transactions of the Woolhope Naturalists' Field Club*, 27 (1930–32)

Moor, C., *Knights of Edward I* (5 vols., Harleian Society, 80–4, 1929–32)

Morris, R.K., 'Decorated Architecture in Herefordshire: Sources, Workshops and Influence', (Courtauld Institute, University of London, PhD thesis, 1972)

— 'The local influence of Hereford Cathedral in the Decorated period', *Transactions of the Woolhope Naturalists' Field Club*, 41 (1973)

— 'The mason of Madley, Allensmore and Eaton Bishop', *Transactions of the Woolhope Naturalists' Field Club*, 41 (1973)

— 'The remodelling of the Hereford aisles', *Journal of the British Archaeological Association*, 38 (1974)

— 'Pembridge and mature Decorated architecture in Herefordshire', *Transactions of the Woolhope Naturalists' Field Club*, 42 (1977)

— 'Late Decorated architecture in northern Herefordshire', *Transactions of the Woolhope Naturalists' Field Club*, 44 (1982)

Mortimer, I., *The Greatest Traitor: the Life of Roger Mortimer, 1st Earl of March, Ruler of England, 1327–30* (London, 2003)

Munns, J. (ed.), *Decorated Revisited. English Architectural Style in Context* (Turnhout, 2017)

Newman, J., and Pevsner, N., *Shropshire* (New Haven and London, 2006)

Pinches, S., *Ledbury. People and Parish before the Reformation* (Chichester, 2010)

Royal Commission on Historical Monuments (England), *Inventory of the Historical Monuments in Herefordshire*, 3 vols. (London, 1931–34)

Saul, N.E., *Lordship and Faith. The English Gentry and the Parish Church in the Middle Ages* (Oxford, 2017)

Tavinor, M. and Bass, I., *Thomas de Cantilupe 700 Years a Saint* (Eardisley, 2020)

Whitehead, D. (ed.), 'Medieval Art, Architecture and Archaeology at Hereford' (*British Archaeological Association Conference Transactions*, 15, 1995)

UNPUBLISHED THESIS

Dryburgh, P.R., 'The career of Roger Mortimer, first earl of March (c. 1287–1330)' (University of Bristol PhD thesis, 2002)

LIST OF ABBREVIATIONS

BL	British Library, London
Brooks and Pevsner,	A. Brooks and N. Pevsner, *Herefordshire* (New Haven and London, 2012)
CIPM	*Calendar of Inquisitions Post Mortem*
CCR	*Calendar of Close Rolls*
CPR	*Calendar of Patent Rolls*
HARC	Herefordshire Archive and Records Centre
Hereford Cathedral	G. Aylmer and J. Tiller (eds.), *Hereford Cathedral. A History* (London, 2000)
TNA	The National Archives, Kew
TWNFC	*Transactions of the Woolhope Naturalists' Field Club*

ENDNOTES

1 Herefordshire and the Decorated Style

1. Shrewsbury enjoyed an income of £530 and St Werburgh's, Chester, of £1,000: J. and C. Hillaby, *Leominster Minster, Priory and Borough, c. 660–1539* (Almeley, 2006), 255.

2. I. Mortimer, *The Greatest Traitor: the Life of Roger Mortimer, 1st Earl of March, Ruler of England, 1327–1330* (London, 2003); P.R. Dryburgh, 'The career of Roger Mortimer, first earl of March (c. 1287–1330)' (University of Bristol PhD thesis, 2002).

3. *CIPM*, vii, no. 711; G.A. Holmes, *The Estates of the Higher Nobility in Fourteenth Century England* (Cambridge, 1957), 10–11.

4. Roger and his wife took possession of the lordships of Trim and Meath in Ireland in 1308. Their English lands were leased to them by Joan's mother for the modest rent of £100 sometime between 1308 and 1322: Holmes, *Estates of the Higher Nobility*, 11–12.

5. G.E. Cokayne and others (eds.), *The Complete Peerage*, 12 vols. in 13 (London, 1910–57), viii, 442–45; Holmes, *Estates of the Higher Nobility*, 14–17.

6. *Complete Peerage*, viii, 445–47.

7. For these two families, see respectively *Complete Peerage*, xii, ii, 250–52; vi, 60–63.

8. For gentry, see below ch. 6

9. N. Coldstream, 'The rise and fall of the Decorated style', in J. Munns (ed.), *Decorated Revisited. English Architectural Style in Context* (Turnhout, 2017), 3–14.

10. N. Coldstream, *The Decorated Style. Architecture and Ornament, 1240–1360*, (London, 1994), 27–59.

11. R.K. Morris, 'The remodelling of the Hereford aisles', *Journal of the British Archaeological Association*, 3rd series, 37 (1974), 21–39.

12. R.K. Morris, 'The Architectural History of the Medieval Cathedral Church', in *Hereford Cathedral*, 218–40. The tower was to fall down in 1786.

2 Building and Builders

1   For the chronology of the building of the cathedral, see R.K. Morris, 'The architectural history of the medieval cathedral church', in *Hereford Cathedral*, 203–40.

2   R.K. Morris, 'Decorated Architecture in Herefordshire: Sources, Workshops, Influence' (Courtauld Institute, University of London, PhD thesis, 1972).

3   For Morris's later views, see especially his 'Architectural history', in *Hereford Cathedral*, 232–40, where the possibility of a mason with links to the court working at Hereford in Edward I's reign is introduced.

4   R.K. Morris, 'The local influence of Hereford Cathedral in the Decorated period', *TWNFC*, 41 (1973), 48–67.

5   R. K. Morris, 'The mason of Madley, Allensmore and Eaton Bishop', *TWNFC*, 41 (1974), 180–97.

6   R.K. Morris, 'Pembridge and mature Decorated architecture in Herefordshire', *TWNFC*, 42 (1977), 129–53.

7   R.K. Morris, 'Late Decorated architecture in northern Herefordshire', *TWNFC*, 44 (1982), 36–58.

8   Morris, 'Pembridge and mature Decorated', 139–40.

9   Morris, 'Local influence of Hereford Cathedral', 52.

10   Morris, 'Pembridge and mature Decorated', 150.

11   J. Newman and N. Pevsner, *Shropshire* (New Haven and London, 2006), p. 22.

12   Brooks and Pevsner, *Herefordshire*, 8. The Cantilupe shrine in the cathedral is probably of sandstone from Fromes Hill, ten miles east of Hereford.

13   A further mark of the distinction of the Wolferlow effigy is the presence at the top of the head of a face cloth held back by the two angels.

14   Pevsner's comment is to be found in only the first edition of his *Herefordshire* (Harmondsworth, 1963), 164. His interpretations have been revised by P. Lindley, 'Retrospective effigies, the past and lies', in D. Whitehead (ed.), 'Medieval Art, Architecture and Archaeology at Hereford' (*British Archaeological Association Conference Transactions*, 15, 1995), 111–21.

15   The Trellech figure, which is now worn, is illustrated in R. Biebrach, *Church Monuments in South Wales, c.1200–1547* (Woodbridge, 2017), fig. 25. I am very grateful to Rhianydd Biebrach for drawing the figure to my attention.

16   The Ledbury monument is discussed further, below, pp. 96–98.

17   B. and M. Gittos, *The Tomb of Blanche Mortimer, Lady Grandisson* (Much Marcle, 2017), 25–26.

18   Work on the screen probably began in 1342: P. Williamson, 'The sculptures of the west front', in M. Swanton (ed.), *Exeter Cathedral. A Celebration* (Exeter, 1991), 74–81.

19   Somewhat optimistically money was being set aside for a new chapter house from as early as 1337: W.W. Capes (ed.), *Charters and Records of Hereford Cathedral* (Hereford, 1908), 220. For the possible date of completion of the chapter house, see Morris, 'Architectural history', in *Hereford Cathedral*, 227.

20   S. Badham, '"A new feire peynted stone": medieval English incised slabs?', *Church Monuments*, 19 (2004), 20–52.

3   The Claims of Piety

1   N.E. Saul, *Lordship and Faith. The English Gentry and the Parish Church in the Middle Ages* (Oxford, 2017), 136.

2   Ibid. 137.

3   Ibid. 140. For a list of chantries and chapels in the north-west of Herefordshire, see P.E.H. Hair, 'Chaplains, chantries and chapels of north-west Herefordshire *c*.1400 (second part)', *TWNFC*, 46 (1989), 246–88.

4   Roofline accents appear to have been popular in Herefordshire, with examples to be seen at Kingsland, Almeley and Allensmore.

5   For Cantilupe's career, see N.D.S. Martin, 'The life of St Thomas of Hereford', in M. Jancey (ed.), *St Thomas Cantilupe, Bishop of Hereford. Essays in his Honour* (Hereford, 1982), 15–19.

6   R.C. Finucane, 'Thomas de Cantilupe [St Thomas of Hereford] (*c*.1220–1282), bishop of Hereford' in online version of the *Oxford Dictionary of National Biography*: http://www.oxforddnb.com.ezproxy01.rhul.ac.uk/view/10.1093/ref:odnb/9780198614128.001.0001/odnb-9780198614128-e-4570?rskey=2d09b5&result=1

7   P.H. Daly, 'The process of canonisation in the thirteenth and early fourteenth centuries', in Jancey (ed.), *St Thomas Cantilupe, Bishop of Hereford*, 125–35.

8   P.E. Morgan, 'The effect of the pilgrim cult of St Thomas Cantilupe on Hereford Cathedral', in Jancey (ed.), *St Thomas Cantilupe, Bishop of Hereford*, 147.

9   Ibid. 141.

10   I.L. Bass, 'Miraculous Marches: the cult of Thomas de Cantilupe and the Mortimers', *Journal of the Mortimer History Society*, 1 (2017), 1–17, at p. 12.

11   Ibid. 13–14.

12   R.C. Finucane, 'Cantilupe as thaumaturge: pilgrims and their 'miracles'', in Jancey (ed.), *St Thomas Cantilupe, Bishop of Hereford*, 138–39.

13 I.L. Bass, 'Miracle in the Marches', *History Today*, 67, 3 (March, 2017), 46.

14 The church at Vowchurch is a more modest one than most of those built by families of knightly rank, taking the form of an aisleless nave and chancel under a continuous roof. What points to the probability of lordly involvement, if only in the form of pump-priming money, is the fact that it is all of one build. Bishop Trilleck rededicated the altars shortly before November 1348: J.H. Parry (ed.), *Registrum Johannis de Trillek, Episcopi Herefordensis* (Canterbury and York Soc., 8, 1912), 143. Churches paid for exclusively by the parishioners usually grew incrementally, a bit at a time.

15 J. Le Neve, *Fasti Ecclesiae Anglicanae, 1300–1541, II, Hereford Diocese*, ed. J.M. Horn (London, 1962), 5, 6, 8, 9, 14, 17, 19, 37, 46, 47, 48.

16 W.W. Capes (ed.), *Registrum Ricardi de Swinfield, Episcopi Herefordensis* (Canterbury and York Soc., 6, 1909), 15, 93, 486. The steward was William de Mortimer.

17 M. Thurlby, *The Herefordshire School of Romanesque Sculpture* (Almeley, 2013), especially chapter 4.

4   The Clergy as Builders

1   Saul, *Lordship and Faith*, 91.

2   J. Newman and N. Pevsner, *Shropshire*, 502, 615.

3   Brooks and Pevsner, *Herefordshire*, 196, 495.

4   Morris, 'Mason of Madley, Allensmore and Eaton Bishop', 180–97, especially 192; Brooks and Pevsner, *Herefordshire*, 223.

5   For a detailed description of the window, see G. Marshall, 'Some remarks on the ancient stained glass in Eaton Bishop church, co. Hereford', *TWNFC*, 24 (1922), 101–14, where it is suggested that the Crucifixion panel is an insertion from another window.

6   A.B. Emden, *A Biographical Register of the University of Oxford to A.D. 1500*, 3 vols., (Oxford, 1957–59), ii, 1329–30. Murimuth is chiefly famous for his *Continuatio Chronicarum*, an important account of the years 1303–1347.

7   A.T. Bannister (ed.), *Registrum Ade de Orleton, Episcopi Herefordensis, A.D. MCCCXVII–MCCCXXVII* (Canterbury and York Soc., 5, 1908), 186–87, 220.

8   Emden, *Biographical Register of the University of Oxford*, ii, 1329–30.

9   S. Pinches, *Ledbury. People and Parish before the Reformation* (Chichester, 2010), 125.

10 Ibid.

11 For the date of the chapel, see Morris, 'Local influence of Hereford Cathedral', 61–63.

12 *CPR 1301–7*, 525. For Ross's career, see Emden, *Biographical Register of the University of Oxford*, iii, 1590–91.

13 *CPR 1301–7*, 434. Silas Taylor, writing in 1655, speaks of 'a small oratory on the north side of the church' with a window in which there were the arms of Talbot: BL, Harley MS 6726, fo. 201r. For Philip, see Le Neve, *Fasti*, 6, 41; and for his institution to Credenhill, R.G. Griffiths and W.W. Capes (eds.), *Registrum Thome de Cantilupo, Episcopi Herefordensis, A.D. MCCLXXV–MCCLXXXII* (Canterbury and York Soc., 2, 1907), 135.

14 BL, Harley MS 6726, fo. 201r.

15 J. Alexander and P. Binski (eds.), *Age of Chivalry. Art in Plantagenet England, 1200–1400* (London, 1987), no. 29.

16 *CPR 1330–4*, 250; *CPR 1345–8*, 67. Boter was treasurer of Hereford from 1348 to 1367: Le Neve, *Fasti*, 10, 41. He was the son of Robert and Joan Boter of the neighbouring parish of Canon Pyon, for whose souls the chaplain was to pray, and for whose benefit in 1345 he obtained permission from the dean and chapter of Hereford to institute a second chantry in the church there: S.H. Martin, 'The chantry at Canon Pyon', *TWNFC*, 35 (1955–57), 162–65.

17 I.L. Bass, '"Who lies beneath?" The Swinfields of Hereford Cathedral', *TWNFC*, 65 (2017), 46–73.

18 W.W. Capes (ed.), *Registrum Ricardi de Swinfield, Episcopi Herefordensis, A.D. MCCLXXXIII–MCCCXVII* (Canterbury and York Soc., 6, 1909), 154, 328.

19 *CPR 1345–8*, 38.

20 Brooks and Pevsner, *Herefordshire*, 497–500.

21 Capes (ed.), *Charters and Records of Hereford Cathedral*, 183.

22 Morris, 'Mason of Madley, Allensmore and Eaton Bishop', 181–91.

23 *Feudal Aids, 1284–1431* (6 vols., London, 1899–1920), ii, 381, 397. Thomas Blount referred to the chapel as the Chilston Chapel in the 1670s: S. Brown, 'The fourteenth-century stained glass of Madley', in Whitehead (ed.), *Medieval Art, Architecture and Archaeology at Hereford*, 122–31, at 127.

24 This much is suggested by the inclusion of Bishop Swinfield among those whose souls were to be prayed for by the two chantry chaplains in the cathedral: *CPR 1345–8*, 38.

25 They were also well connected. Among those who witnessed the transference of the family's advowson of Dinedor as endowment for the chantry in the cathedral were Sir Peter de Grandison, Sir Roger Chandos and Sir Richard de Pembridge: Capes (ed.), *Charters and Records of Hereford Cathedral*, 223–24.

5   The Unlikely Patrons: The Mortimers

1   R.R. Davies, *Lordship and Society in the March of Wales, 1282–1400* (Oxford, 1978), 53–54.

2   Holmes, *Estates of the Higher Nobility*, 10–15.

3   M.W. Beresford and H.P.R. Finberg, *English Medieval Boroughs. A Handlist*, David and Charles (Newton Abbot, 1973), 123.

4   The marriage at Pembridge was recorded in the Wigmore chronicle: P.M. Remfry (ed.), *The Wigmore Chronicle, 1066–1377* (Shrewsbury, 2013), 66.

5   The nave is conceived in the form of a broad single cell, without aisles: Brooks and Pevsner, *Herefordshire*, 539.

6   J. Newman and N. Pevsner, *Shropshire*, 438.

7   *CPR 1327–30*, 343.

8   Whether the chantry ever lived up to its founder's original expectations is another matter. Given the instability of the family's fortunes in the years after his death, it is highly unlikely that the establishment ever attained its full strength. Heraldry featured strongly in the stained glass windows. In 1655 there were Mortimer arms remaining in the chancel windows, which Silas Taylor recorded: BL, Harley MS 6726, fo. 67v.

9   Newman and Pevsner, *Shropshire*, 214.

10   Morris, 'Late Decorated architecture', 36-58; G. Marshall, 'The church of Richard's Castle, co. Hereford', *TWNFC*, 25 (1924–26), 114–18.

11   Newman and Pevsner, *Shropshire*, 22, 193. Sir Hugh was to live on until 1372: his death at Luton, another of his manors, was recorded by the Wigmore chronicler (*Wigmore Chronicle*, 93).

12   K. Aston and P. Klein, *A walk round the church of St Mary the Virgin, Pembridge, Herefordshire* (Pembridge, 2005), 12–13.

13   Morris, 'Pembridge and mature Decorated', 129–53, at 131.

14   Morris, 'Late Decorated architecture', 36–58, at pp. 53–57; G. Marshall, 'Notes on Kingsland church, Herefordshire', *TWNFC*, 27 (1930–32), 21–28.

15   BL, Add MS 17458, fo. 67r (David Powell's notes).

16   C. Hopkinson, 'The Mortimers of Wigmore, 1282–1330', *TWNFC*, 48 (1995), 303–34, at 321.

17   The process of updating the essentially late twelfth-century church to provide improved accommodation for family burials was only undertaken in the second half of the century: Brooks and Pevsner, *Herefordshire*, 81.

18   *CIPM*, 7, no. 711; *Feudal Aids*, ii, 387; Holmes, *Estates of the Higher Nobility*, 11.

19   *CIPM*, 10, no, 307. Joan held the three manors of Pembridge, Kingsland and Orleton for life by demise from her grandson Roger, the second earl: *CPR 1345–8*, 349.

20   Morris, 'Late Decorated architecture', 56.

21   G. Marshall, 'Notes on Kingsland church', 21–28.

22   C.E. Long (ed.) with new introduction by I. Roy, *Richard Symonds's Diary of the Marches of the Royal Army*, Camden Classic Reprints, 3 (Cambridge, 1997), 202.

23   BL, Add. MS 17458, fo. 67r. The arms of de Braose refer to the marriage of Roger Mortimer (d.1282) to Maud, eldest daughter and coheir of William de Braose. This Roger, the grandfather of the first earl, had died at Kingsland: *Complete Peerage*, ix, 280.

24   Hume, *On the Trail of the Mortimers*, 80.

6   The Gentry and the Townsmen

1   Two exceptions are the chancels at Dilwyn and Lyonshall, both built by Wormsley priory.

2   The Croft family's interest in the church is illustrated by John de Croft's evidence at the proof of age of John Tyrel in 1360, in which he describes recalling the child's baptism because his sister had died on the same day, and he had had her death entered in the obits list in the missal in the church: *CIPM*, 10, no. 642. The recollection may be embroidered, but the act described would have carried conviction to the extent that it was characteristic of gentry behaviour.

3   The church was built, probably in her widowhood, by Sybil, the wife of Sir Grimbald Pauncefot who had died in 1287. It was consecrated in 1303: R. Scourfield and R. Haslam, *Powys: Montgomeryshire, Radnorshire and Breconshire* (New Haven and London, 2013), 469. Sibyl is buried in a recess on the honorific north side of the chancel and her husband in a recess opposite.

4   At Fownhope the former south chapel was later to be absorbed into an expanded aisle, while at Credenhill the north chapel has since been demolished. At Almeley there are non-projecting transepts: see, respectively, *Inventory*, ii, 80–82; ii, 64–67; iii, 4–7.

5   The new chantry was established in the name of two local men, Roger Berde and John Luntley of Newton in Dilwyn, who, together in 1392, made over lands for the endowment of a chantry in what they termed the Lady chapel of the church – that is to say, the north transept (*CPR 1391–96*, 119). In the light of the men's obscurity it seems likely that they were acting as feoffees for the de la Bere family, whose presence in the church was increasing in the second half of the

century. At the west end of the nave is a fragmentary, displaced tomb slab, probably originally in the chapel, which bears a portion of a shield bearing the family's arms, and in the chancel there was a stained glass panel, now lost but recorded by both Symonds and Taylor, of a kneeling knight with the same arms on his breastplate, *c.*1380–90: BL, Harley MS 944, fo. 59r; BL, Harley MS 6726, fo 183v; T. Dingley, *History from Marble*, ii, ed. T.E. Winnington (Camden Soc., old series 97, 1868), fos. 266, 267. The de la Beres had acquired the manor of Alton in Dilwyn by the 1380s (*CIPM*, xv, no. 791); their two main properties were the manors of Stretford and Kinnersley, close by. It is most likely that the chapel had originally been built by the Tyrels, lords of one of the manors in the village, as Symonds recorded the arms of Tyrel at the foot of the chapel's north window: C.E. Long (ed.), *Richard Symonds's Diary of the Marches of the Royal Army* (Camden Soc., old series 74 (1859), 265. The Tyrels had died out in the male line in 1380, and appear anyway to have been residing chiefly on their lands in other counties well before then: *CIPM*, 11, no. 547; xv, nos. 420–26.

6   The tombs, each showing a lawyer and his wife, were moved from the transept to the north-west corner of the nave by 1900, and are now in the chancel. The north transept was a part of the church associated with the manor of Marston in Pembridge: J.B. Hewitt, 'Pembridge church, Herefordshire', *TWNFC*, 14 (1900–02), 141–44, at 143. The couples commemorated were identified by Symonds in the 1640s as members of the Gour family: Long (ed.), *Richard Symonds's Diary*, 203. They are probably Nicholas Gour and his wife, *c.* 1370, and their son, John, and his wife, *c.* 1380. Both generations of the family had Mortimer connections: N.E. Saul, *English Church Monuments in the Middle Ages: History and Representation* (Oxford, 2009), 245–46, 275–76.

7   TNA, C143/84/3, an inquisition *ad quod damnum* for the transfer of the advowson of King's Pyon to Wormsley priory; Dugdale, *Monasticon Anglicanum*, VI, i, 403.

8   Brooks and Pevsner, *Herefordshire*, 390. The tower also appears to be of the fourteenth century.

9   In the *taxatio* of Pope Nicholas IV the living was valued at £15 6s 8d: https://www.dhi.ac.uk/taxatio/benkey?benkey=HE.HE.WE.02

10   The inquisition taken on the death of Roger Mortimer, earl of March (d.1398), records half a knight's fee formerly held of the late earl at King's Pyon by Hugh Mortimer: *CIPM*, 17, no. 1213 (446). As the manor was seemingly still held by the Eylesfords at the time, the presence of a Mortimer knight in the parish can only be accounted for on the assumption that he was the second husband of an Eylesford widow.

11   *Complete Peerage*, vi, 60–67; xii, ii, 246–51.

12   Weobley was one of Verdons' manors: *Feudal Aids*, ii, 387. For the heraldic glass at Ludlow, see Morris, 'Local influence of Hereford Cathedral', 57.

13   Sir William Devereux (d.1314) lost the family *caput* of Lyonshall, and his family were subsequently to settle at Bodenham, where Sir Stephen, probably a grandson, was lord in Edward II's reign (*Complete Peerage*, iv, 302-3; *Feudal Aids*, ii, 384). The church is a fine mainly fourteenth-century building. Dingley illustrates a later fourteenth-century alabaster effigy of a Devereux knight on a tomb chest, now lost: Dingley, *History from Marble*, i, fo. ccxxxvi). The effigy had earlier been noted by Taylor: BL, Harley MS 6726, fo. 91d.

14   Chandos, whose main seat was Snodhill castle in Peterchurch, was summoned to parliament from 1337 to his death in 1353 but was the only member of his family to receive the honour: *Complete Peerage*, iii, 147–48. His second wife, whom he married before 1315, was Maud, widow of the wealthy Somerset knight, Sir Nicholas Pointz; for her dower lands, see *CCR 1313–18*, 168. Chandos founded a chantry in Fownhope church: *CPR 1317–21*, 408.

15   For the family's descent, see R.W. Eyton, *The Antiquities of Shropshire*, 12 vols., ed. J.R. Smith (London, 1854–61), iii, 44, and for their lands, C. Moor, *Knights of Edward I* (5 vols., Harleian Soc., 80–84, 1929-32), iii, 209–10; *CIPM*, 13, no. 194.

16   For Crickhowell, see Scourfield and Haslam, *Powys: Montgomeryshire, Radnorshire and Breconshire*, 469–70. The Pauncefots were also responsible for the new south aisle at Much Cowarne, where Sir Grimbald (d.1314) was buried and is commemorated by an effigy, now badly mutilated. Sir Robert de la Bere was active between *c*.1305 and *c*.1335 and was succeeded by his son, Sir John, who died *c*.1340–50. John's son in turn, Sir Richard, married Sybil, the daughter and heiress of John de Kinnersley, and through her inherited the manor of Kinnersley: G. Marshall, 'Stretford church, co. Hereford', *TWNFC*, 1930–32, 11–20.

17   In 1357 Sir Richard de la Bere obtained from the king the grant of a weekly market at Kinnersley and a yearly fair there each 24 and 25 July (*Cal. Charter Rolls 1341–1417*, 55).

18   Perhaps because of their limited landholdings members of neither family were active in office-holding in the county, although on one occasion, in 1307, Hugh de Kinnersley was elected a member of parliament. The de Kinnersleys became extinct in the male line in the 1340s, when their manor of Kinnersley was taken over by the de la Beres of Stretford. For brief notes on the Sarnesfield family, see G. Marshall, 'Monumental inscriptions at Sarnesfield, Co. Hereford', *The Genealogist*, new series 12 (1896), 7–18, at 7.

19   Capes (ed.), *Reg. Swinfield*, 76–77, 348.

20 Ibid. 77–78.

21 As Tyrel's arms were once in the north window of the north chapel, he may have been the builder of that part of the church: Long (ed.), *Symonds's Diary*, 265. His tomb effigy, however, occupies a position of honour in a recess on the north side of the chancel; for his career, see Moor, *Knights of Edward 1*, v, 68–69. Chandos was in Hereford's retinue at the Dunstable tournament of 1309: A. Tomkinson, 'Retinues at the tournament of Dunstable', *English Historical Review*, 74 (1959), 73; it was through Hereford's intercession that he obtained the royal mortmain licence for his chantry at Fownhope: *CPR 1317–21*, 408.

22 *List of Sheriffs for England and Wales* (PRO Lists and Indexes, 9, 1898), 59; *Return of Members of Parliament*, i (House of Commons, 1878), 21, 46, 9, 24, 16, 27, 55, 64.

23 *CPR 1338–40*, 502; *CPR 1340–3*, 155; *CPR 1343–5*, 395.

24 *CPR 1340–3*, 410; *CPR 1345–8*, 418. At Yazor Clanvow's transeptal chantry chapel forms the principal remaining part of the old Yazor church, which is now ruinous: Brooks and Pevsner, *Herefordshire*, 692.

25 TNA, C67/16 mm. 2, 4, 11, 12; TNA, C81/1725/32; H. Gough (ed.), *Scotland in 1298*, (Paisley, 1888), 229.

26 G. Wrottesley (ed.), *Crécy and Calais from the Original Records in the Public Record Office* (London, 1898), 114.

27 For the knights' record in office-holding, see above. More details of their careers may be found in the entries, arranged alphabetically, in Moor, *Knights of Edward 1*.

28 *CIPM*, 4, no. 235 (p. 166); Moor, *Knights of Edward I*, iv, p. 62; *CCR 1307–13*, 98; *CIPM*, 5, no. 57 (p. 24); *CIPM*, 17, no. 1213; J.S. Roskell, 'Sir Peter de la Mare, Speaker of the Commons in Parliament in 1376 and 1377', in his *Parliament and Politics in Late Medieval England* (London, 1981), 1–14.

29 Dugdale, *Monasticon Anglicanum*, VI, i, 352.

30 BL, Harley MS 1240, fos. 39v, 43d, 44r. For the Mortimer retinue, see Dryburgh, 'The career of Roger Mortimer, 1st earl of March (c. 1287–1330)', chapter 5.

31 BL, Harley MS 1240, fo. 39v.

32 *CPR 1307–13*, 283. In May 1317, in the course of Mortimer's second visit to Ireland, Croft was seized and killed by the de Lacys, Mortimer's enemies, when he attempted to deliver to them letters ordering their submission to his master: Mortimer, *The Greatest Traitor*, 85.

33 *CPR 1321–4*, 17, 19.

34   *CCR 1318–23*, 433: two orders for the restoration of lands seized by the king, dated 23 and 25 March 1322, in the wake of the king's victory over the rebels at Boroughbridge, suggesting that the men had already made their submissions by then. Aymer Pauncefot was to secure restoration on condition that he perform military service in Gascony: *Parliamentary Writs*, II, ii, 692. Two other Herefordshire knights, Gilbert Talbot and Richard de Pembridge, were likewise pardoned on the same condition, pointing to their involvement in the revolt even though they do not appear in the lists of those whose lands were seized: ibid.

35   The present Lingen church is mostly a rebuilding of 1890. A drawing of its predecessor, however, shows it to have been a simple structure of seemingly early date, without aisles and with nave and chancel under a single roof. There is no evidence of any early fourteenth-century features: Hereford Library, Walter Pilley Collection, 'Churches of Herefordshire', 1882.

36   For the Hereford churches, see Brooks and Pevsner, *Herefordshire*, 306–8, 311–12.

37   For these churches, see respectively ibid., 444–45, 415–18, 569–70.

38   *CPR 1301–7*, 525.

39   Pinches, *Ledbury. People and Parish*, 126.

40   *CPR 1354–8*, 49–50; *CPR 1370–4*, 372; BL, Harley MS 6726, fo. 173d.

41   Pinches, *Ledbury. People and Parish*, 127.

42   R.M. Haines, *The Church and Politics in Fourteenth-Century England. The Career of Adam Orleton, c. 1275–1345* (Cambridge, 1978), 1–2.

7 Paying the Bills

1   For these examples, see L.F. Salzman, *Building in England down to 1540* (Oxford, 2nd edn., 1997), 437–38, 482–83, 487–90. The cost for the rebuilding of Catterick excluded the tower and the vestry.

2   Morgan, 'The effect of the pilgrim cult', in Jancey (ed.), *St Thomas Cantilupe, Bishop of Hereford*, 147.

3   P. Binski, *Gothic Wonder. Art, Artifice and the Decorated Style, 1290–1350* (New Haven and London, 2014), 84–85.

4   TNA, SC6/1145/16. Sir Richard had suffered loss of property as a result of his involvement in the rebellion against Edward II.

5   These are not reproduced in the calendared inquisitions in *CIPM*, in which it is only noted if a full extent was drawn up. Unfortunately, there are very few extents for members of the Herefordshire knightly class, as most of these men did not hold in chief; there is not one, for example, for Sir Richard de Pembridge, with which the partial account in TNA, SC6/1145/16 might be compared.

6   TNA, C135/45/22. The inquisitions, drawn up in 1336 two years after Margaret's death, are calendared in *CIPM*, vii, no. 711. For Margaret's dower assignment, see Holmes, *Estates of the Higher Nobility*, 11–12.

7   At her death Margaret was recorded as holding the manor of Bewdley (Worcs) and a third of the manors of Bridgwater (Som.) and Long Crendon (Bucks): *CIPM*, vii, no. 711, these being properties that she held in chief. Two extents were drawn up of her manor of Bewdley, the first in June 1336 placing an unrealistically low valuation on the property, and the second, ordered three months later presumably in response to the low initial valuation, still recording a minimalist figure: a mere £5 1s 8d per annum: TNA, C135/45/22. Since Bewdley was developing proto-urban characteristics at this time, a value of £5 is hardly credible.

8   E. Power, *The Wool Trade in English Medieval History* (Oxford, 1941), p. 21.

9   Ibid., p. 23.

10   *CPR 1334–8*, 480–83.

11   T.H. Lloyd, *The Movement of Wool Prices in Medieval England* (Cambridge: Economic History Review Supplement, 6, 1973), 10–11.

12   Because the clips were disposed of in this way, income from wool does not appear in the extents in Margaret's inquisition of 1334: TNA, C135/45/22.

13   Long (ed.), *Richard Symonds's Diary*, 268.

8   The End of It All

1   P.E. Morgan, 'The effect of the pilgrim cult of St Thomas Cantilupe on Hereford Cathedral', in Jancey (ed.), *St Thomas Cantilupe, Bishop of Hereford*, 148, 149.

2   Morgan, 'Effect of the pilgrim cult', 151.

3   Saul, *Lordship and Faith*, 140.

4   Although it is apparent from the tomb recess in the south wall and the presence of a piscina in the corner that the aisle was built to accommodate a chantry chapel, there is no record of any chantry foundation in the church – a reminder, if any were needed, of the incompleteness of our knowledge of these foundations.

5   W.J. Dohar, *The Black Death and Pastoral Leadership. The Diocese of Hereford in the Fourteenth Century* (Philadelphia, 1995), 38.

6   Dohar, *Black Death and Pastoral Leadership*, 42.

7   HARC, F78/1/5.

8   HARC, A31/7; A31/25.

9   The problem can be picked up especially in the accounts of properties, such as the manor and banlieu of Wigmore, the income from which was largely drawn from these sources: BL, Egerton Roll 8362.

10   G. Byng, *Church Building and Society in the Later Middle Ages* (Cambridge, 2017), 26–28.

11   R. Morris, *Cathedrals and Abbeys of England and Wales. The Building Church, 600–1540* (London,1979), 180.

12   T.H. Lloyd, *Movement of Wool Prices*, 11.

INDEX

All the places referred to are in Herefordshire unless otherwise indicated

Also from LOGASTON PRESS (www.logastonpress.co.uk)

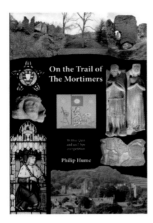

On the Trail of the Mortimers
Philip Hume
144 pages, 234 × 156 mm
75 colour photographs, as well as maps and family trees
ISBN: 978-1-910839-04-1
Paperback with flaps, £7.50

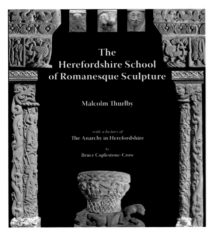

The Herefordshire School of Romanesque Sculpture
Malcolm Thurlby
320 pages, 240 × 210 mm
400 colour illustrations
ISBN: 978-1-906663-72-8
Paperback with flaps, £17.50

Thomas de Cantilupe – 700 Years a Saint
St Thomas of Hereford
Compiled by the Dean of Hereford Cathedral,
the Very Reverend Michael Tavinor, and Dr Ian Bass
96 pages, 210 × 148 mm
80 colour illustrations
ISBN: 978-1-910839-41-6
Paperback, £7.50